Teach!
Change!
Empower!

This book is dedicated to Dr. Gloria W. Grant. Gloria's inherent caring about all children, particularly those who are poor, second-language learners, of color, and disenfranchised was a source of inspiration to her colleagues, friends, students, and family. Her teaching was an action pedagogy in mentoring other colleagues to make their teaching and learning more inclusive. This publication is a small effort to perpetuate her legacy of love and caring of children, as well as her persistence in calling on educators to show responsibility and love in teaching.

Teach!
Change!
Empower!

SOLUTIONS FOR CLOSING THE ACHIEVEMENT GAPS

CARL A. GRANT

CORWIN
A SAGE Company

For information:

 Corwin
A SAGE Company
2455 Teller Road
Mathura Road,
Thousand Oaks, California 91320
(800) 233-9936
Fax: (800) 417-2466
www.corwinpress.com

SAGE Ltd.
1 Oliver's Yard
55 City Road
London EC1Y 1SP
United Kingdom

SAGE India Pvt. Ltd.
B 1/I 1 Mohan Cooperative
Industrial Area
New Delhi 110 044
India

SAGE Asia-Pacific Pte. Ltd.
33 Pekin Street #02-01
Far East Square
Singapore 048763

Printed in the United States of America.

Library of Congress Cataloging-in-Publication Data

Grant, Carl A.
Teach! change! empower!: Solutions for closing the achievement gaps/Carl A. Grant.
    p. cm.
Includes bibliographical references and index.
ISBN 978-1-4129-7648-0 (cloth)
ISBN 978-1-4129-7649-7 (pbk.)
    1. Effective teaching. 2. Teachers—Professional relationships. 3. Academic achievement.
I. Title.

LB1025.3.G72 2009
371.102—dc22   2009023354

This book is printed on acid-free paper.

09   10   11   12   13   10   9   8   7   6   5   4   3   2   1

Acquisitions Editor:	Dan Alpert
Associate Editor:	Megan Bedell
Production Editor:	Eric Garner
Copy Editor:	Kathryn Pompy
Typesetter:	C&M Digitals (P) Ltd.
Proofreader:	Charlotte Waisner
Indexer:	Jean Casalegno
Cover Designer:	Rose Storey
Graphic Designer:	Brian Bello

Contents

Preface

The world in which most adult Americans grew to maturity no longer exists. The Cold War is over. The domestic economy is global. The melting pot is boiling over. Our world is in flux. The arrival of the twenty-first century has ushered in not simply a new millennium but also a completely new and different globe (American Council of Education [ACE], 1995, p. 3; Friedman, 2008). Linking education to this new world, Rhode (2006) argues, "Academic institutions—universities, high schools, middle schools and elementary schools—are crucial in creating the informed citizens essential to democratic self-governance and the skilled workforce essential for prosperity in a competitive global economy" (p. 3). In addition, our legally free and fair society requires that academic institutions offer all children, regardless of race/ethnicity, income, geographic location, or language, the knowledge and skills to enable them to reach their fullest potential and have a flourishing life; by this, I mean a thriving and fulfilling life both inside and outside the bounds of the economy. In this sense, schools and teachers bear primary responsibility for creating equal opportunity for all (Rocha & Sharkey, 2007).

Schools and teachers—individually and collectively—have, especially since the 1960s, made efforts to accomplish this goal. However, many of the efforts have fallen short because they were often too narrowly focused in implementing staff development sessions dealing with the latest educational fad (e.g., assertive discipline) or they were too heavy handed (e.g., No Child Left Behind [NCLB]) in limiting teachers' participation in the curriculum and pedagogical decision making.

For the most part, student achievement has increased for all students during the past decade; the achievement gap between both White students and students of color as well as students from low socioeconomic homes and those from middle to upper socioeconomic homes remains a complex, persistent problem (National Education Association, 2004). Also, since the National Commission on Excellence in Education's publication of *A Nation at Risk* in 1983, the academic achievement gap has created a storm of controversy at all levels of government and in all sectors of civil society. The achievement gap and the controversy surrounding it as well as the increased cultural, racial, and socioeconomic diversity in the United States and the influence of globalization demands that teachers come to teaching with more and different knowledge and skills, as well as a social justice orientation.

Finally, *Teach! Change! Empower!* brings the researched and best-practice ideas together that educators argue are critical for eliminating the academic achievement gap and that make the teaching/learning experience more rewarding for both teachers and students. *Teach! Change! Empower!* puts into practice ideas that have been vetted through discussion of diversity and power that challenge the achievement gaps: culturally relevant and rigorous curriculum, caring with a sociopolitical consciousness, community and culture of learning, cooperative professional development, democratic student involvement, high-quality teaching, and personal and program performance accountability. Each of the ten chapters uses one or more of these seven tested and researched ideas to help teachers eliminate the achievement gap in their classroom.

TEACHER INVESTMENT

Education (i.e., excellent public education) will not survive for your children and grandchildren if teachers do not significantly invest their energy and time in *good, old-fashioned teaching.* Miss Wilson, first grade, Mrs. Austin, fifth grade, Mrs. Jewel, eighth grade, and all my other teachers *demanded* that I learn that lesson and finish every assignment; that I return homework, completed, with the pages neat and clean; and that I sit or stand up straight when I answered a question.

Teach! Change! Empower! is written for teachers who wish to engage in good public education; it is written to teach those who want to teach how to be effective for all students. While it is particularly great for teacher/leaders, teachers participating in staff development or for teachers who are working to become mentor teachers, the book effectively supports *all* teachers who are working to close the achievement gap and to assist students who are challenged by other gaps (e.g., economic, health) in classrooms where changes in student demographics are underway and in schools (especially in urban areas) where an increase in school segregation is taking place.

I pay attention to *gaps* in the plural because teachers deal with more gaps than merely achievement. In some classrooms, teachers deal with poverty and health needs by, for example, recommending and facilitating access to social resources. I recognize that, in some schools, affirming diversity is often seen as taking time away from a "back-to-the-basics" emphasis and meeting the demands of the state curriculum standards. That said, I, along with an increasing number of teachers and researchers, believe that affirming and promoting diversity is integral to—and not a detractor from—closing the achievement gap. My belief is based on simple logic. For decades, if not centuries, students of color in U.S. schools have lagged behind White students. This difference in school performance between students of color and White students has been attributed to reasons such as innate IQ differences, cultural deficiencies, home background, social and economic disadvantage, and so forth. Policy and programmatic responses to eliminate these perceived reason(s) for achievement gaps, while often well meaning, for the most part marginalize or ignore (not appreciate) the diversity of the students. They, either directly or implicitly, see diversity as the cause of academic under-achievement rather than *part of the solution*. This book learns from those mistakes and instead brings together both achievement and the affirmation of diversity, which is the foundational idea of culturally relevant pedagogy and fundamental to multicultural education.

This book is designed to encourage and facilitate positive learning experiences. It includes activities to promote social and professional growth. Through reading the book and participating in the activities, teachers will become more informed about teaching, themselves, and their students, as well as more knowledgeable about how other teachers and staff members can participate in closing the academic achievement gap.

The personal and educational change that I am calling for demands, not a short one- or two-hour event but short blocks of time over an extended period (e.g., a semester or school year). It is change that invites lifelong learning both in ourselves as individual teachers and in the institutions where we work. By participating in this learning process, teachers demonstrate unselfish and caring action as they undertake it in the best interests of their students. I am very much aware that structural barriers exist and that teachers will have a difficult time doing this work on their own; I am aware that some schools, districts, and policies oppose such work. Nevertheless, our children deserve a much better education than they've been receiving; the quality of their tomorrow depends on it. If teachers work on these changes with the support of other colleagues, they can become a force for change.

Acknowledgments

I wish to thank Vonzell Agosto and Ronald Jetty, who read and commented on earlier drafts. Melissa Gibson, Ruth Gurgel, and Connie North's scholarly contributions, suggestions, and statements of positive motivation were a major source of encouragement. The ideas and suggestions from the teachers and grad students in Curriculum & Instruction 860: Supervision of Student Teachers during the summer of 2007 is greatly appreciated. I am indeed indebted to Jennifer Austin who worked tirelessly on some of the technical aspects of the manuscript. Finally, a huge thanks to my colleague professor Michael Thomas, whose work on the text boxes, graphs, and other details was exceptional.

PUBLISHER'S ACKNOWLEDGEMENTS

Corwin greatly acknowledges the following reviewers:

Paul C. Gorski, Founder
EdChange, Fairfax, VA

Barbara Heuberger Rose, Associate Professor
Department of Teacher Education, Miami University, Oxford, OH

Deborah L. Misiag, Instructional Facilitator
Howard County Public School System, Howard County, MD

Maria Whittemore, Minority Achievement Coordinator
Frederick County Public Schools, Frederick, MD

Peter T. Wilson, President
Education Equity Consultants, LLC, St. Louis, MO

About the Author

Carl A. Grant is Hoefs-Bascom Professor of teacher education in the Department of Curriculum and Instruction at the University of Wisconsin–Madison. His work for more than thirty years has been with teachers and administrators who commit to improve students' achievement, enrich their knowledge and skill set in multicultural social justice, culturally responsive curriculum development, and teaching. He has written several books and many articles for teachers that address student achievement, curriculum development, teaching strategies, and parent-teacher engagement.

Getting the Most Out of the Book

This book is organized into three parts: The Harder Work of Teaching, The Change Process, and Change/Solutions in Practice. Each part contains several chapters, and each chapter includes activities to be completed over a short period of time, such as a week or two. Throughout the book are interactive activities, which include reflections, taking action, dialoguing with colleagues, and journaling. Additionally, at the end of each chapter there is an Action Plan to help you develop a plan of action and timeline for implementing practices that will work toward the closure of the academic achievement gap and affirming diversity. In order not to interrupt teachers' learning process, I have placed pertinent—but parenthetical—background information in the "Do You Know?" sections.

To get the most out of this book, teachers should work in groups of two or three. It will be helpful if the group members' cultural backgrounds differ. In addition, for the work to be effective (to all), teachers must be serious in their willingness to be honest. At times, some of the reflections and activities may be uncomfortable or a bit painful in that they may lead to some personal revelations that you would rather ignore or remain blind to; but we will see them, and we will make changes only if we are willing to honestly assess ourselves, our beliefs, and our practices.

In sum, this book is designed to facilitate constructive engagement among professionals who are concerned about the state of public education, who wish to close the achievement gap, and who, in the process, wish to minimize harmful conflicts as well as encourage honesty and respect. I wrote the book from the point of view that everyone can (and should) contribute to resolving social and educational problems. No one has all the answers; in fact, we are all on a steep learning curve.

Therefore, we must become a community of learners. I am very optimistic because I believe the following to be true:

- Teaching can be a fantastic experience.
- Teachers want to help all students succeed to their highest potential.
- The present generation of teachers has the greatest possibility to be successful with closing achievement gaps and addressing issues of diversity.

My hope is that by reading this book and engaging in the activities, teacher groups will develop new ways of thinking and acting that will enable them to help students maintain a positive disposition while acquiring the tools needed to close the achievement gap. Please remember:

Never doubt that a small group of thoughtful, committed citizens can change the world. Indeed, it is the only thing that ever has.

—Margaret Mead

Part I

The Harder Work of Teaching

I came to understand that teaching is hard and that being smart and well educated doesn't necessarily mean one will be good at it.

—Chester E. Finn (2008, p. 24)

Are you ready to join the harder work club? Public education needs you! When correctly characterized, teaching is hard work, and better teaching is even harder work. One of the few things popular authors and filmmakers get right about teachers and teaching is that it is challenging and rewarding work. The even harder work of better teachers is illustrated in the work of many teachers, including those whose harder work has been publicly recognized and celebrated: Anne Sullivan's work with Helen Keller; Anna Julia Cooper's work with the students at Washington High School (M Street School); Sylvia Ashton Warner's organic teaching method with Maori children; Herb Kohl's work in *36 Children* to debunk the myth that educational failure is the students' fault; and Brian Schultz's work with students in an urban school in Chicago.

Teaching as harder work is not a New Age phenomena. From the time of Homer, Plato, Confucius, and Rousseau, teachers teaching students to participate and contribute to a better way of life has been harder work. Today, in the twenty-first century, teaching is harder work because, more than at any other time in history, students face complexities and challenges that are not only local but also global, which makes teaching harder; teachers are also called upon to teach the most basic concepts of manners and politeness as well as, in many cases, to even be the "rock" in students' lives.

I spend a good deal of time in schools; much of that time is spent talking with teachers and students. After I am at a school for a while and teachers get to know me as someone they can trust—that is, someone who will not take their comments to the principal or other teachers or someone who will not think less of them when they are honest—I am usually asked by a teacher (or teachers), "What can I do to better help my students?" I especially hear this question when the students are from low socioeconomic homes, families of color, or their native language is not English. Most teachers ask me this question because they genuinely want to close achievement gaps. However, in concert with this question, I also hear teachers' additional statements about dissatisfaction over accountability mandates, limited resources, annoyance with being rebuked in the media, lack of professional commitment by some staff members, anxiety over parent-teacher relations, and kids not wanting to learn. In short, I hear a description of just how harder teaching is.

Sometimes the teachers' questions and statements are rhetorical. They emerge from frustration or the need to vent. Sometimes the teachers' questions or statements are a plea for help and support. At other times, the questions are a challenge to this former teacher and now university professor because I have the privilege to move in and out of classrooms as well as faculty and grade-level meetings while observing, interviewing, and chatting with teachers. To them, my job seems so much easier than theirs.

It is because of the teachers' questions about the achievement gap (and the influence of the other gaps) and the contextual statements accompanying these questions and comments that I write this book, and while doing so, pull no punches—that is, I am honest and blunt because I am concerned about both children and public education. I say to my teacher/friends, in some ways the days and nights I put into writing this book—while maybe not as hard as teaching a class of 25 (or more) anxious fifth graders or tenth graders—were still a tough challenge. The book is my way of giving back for the privilege I have had as a university-based educator of picking teachers', administrators', students', and parents' brains about closing the achievement gap and affirming diversity. In listening well while doing this, I believe that I have written a book that will help accomplish closing that gap and affirming diversity if teachers stick to the plan, a plan that sometimes asks you to work alone and sometimes encourages you to work with teacher/friends; a plan that is up-to-date, informative, and blunt about issues regarding achievement and affirming diversity; a plan that provides action plans for you to be reflective and responsive; a plan that is supportive while you deal with change/transition; and a plan that will provide you with "full blown tested" lessons for you to see how to make good teaching better and how to close the achievement gaps, affirm diversity, and be pleased about choosing teaching as a career.

1 The Achievement Gap

It's not just going to school but learning something while there that matters.

—Hanushek, Levy, and Kohtaru (2008)

While reading the title of this book—*Teach! Change! Empower!*—some of you may have declared, "I don't need another publication telling me about student achievement and diversity." You may say this because you have had it with discussions in the media, at conferences, in faculty meetings, and in the teachers' lounge about legislation, official decrees demanding high-stakes testing, the need for higher student achievement, and increased attention to diversity. In addition, you are angry—OK, maybe not angry, but definitely annoyed—because the discussions, for the most part, are neither kind nor understanding of teachers. Teachers and principals are presented as the primary culprits for what is wrong in schools (and much of U.S. society).

It is true that these discussions are everywhere; they are not kind to teachers and many are unfair. However, you also know that they will continue until schools undergo reforms to eliminate the achievement gap. Even if everyone who is raising questions were silent, the achievement gap and the difficult challenges schools face affirming diversity would not go away.

WHAT IS THE ACHIEVEMENT GAP AND WHY MUST IT BE ELIMINATED?

The achievement gap is the difference between the academic performance of poor students and wealthy students, between minority and nonminority students, between students who are in special education and those who are not, and between second-language learners and first-language learners (McCall, Hauser, Kingsbury, Cronin & Houser, 2006). It illustrates restricted life chances and choices, chances and choices that will be cut short for increasing numbers of poor and minority children by virtue of their educational "failures." In the 21st century, education, knowledge, and technological training are among the most valuable assets a citizen can have to find employment and to act as a thoughtful, social, responsive, and reflective individual. Thus, addressing achievement gap is critical for enabling students to reach their fullest potential and to having a flourishing life, both inside and outside the bounds of the economy.

The National Governors Association (NGA) Center for Best Practices (2007) states that the achievement gap is one of the most pressing education policy challenges that states currently face. Olson (2007); Jencks and Phillips (1998); Jacobsen, Olsen, Rice, Sweetland, and Ralph (2001); Farkas (2004); McCall et al. (2006); Rothstein (2004); and Noguera and Wang (2006) all contend that differences in educational performance and attainment between Whites, Blacks, and other students of color continue to be central to inequality in the United States. Numerous research studies (e.g., Olson, 2007; Phillips, Crouse, & Ralph, 1998; Jacobsen et al., 2001; McCall et al., 2006) also report that during every year of schooling, Blacks and Latinos learn less than White students.

Olson (2007) uses results from the National Assessment of Educational Progress (NAEP), also known as "the nation's report card," to measure the progress that states have made in raising student achievement in elementary and secondary schools over past decades. Olson states that, as measured by the NAEP, or the nation's report card, "When looked at over that longer time period student achievement has gotten better"(p. 42) with mathematics scores in particular improving for low-income Black and Latino students. But reading achievement "has barely budged since 1992" and high school achievement remains "flat" (p. 42). Moreover, the report emphasized that "achievement gaps based on race and class remain daunting," noting that, near the end of high school, Black and Latino students "have reading and math skills that are virtually the same as those of eighth graders" (p. 42). Ironically, although Black students start elementary school only one year behind White students in vocabulary knowledge, they finish high school approximately four years behind

White students in math and reading achievement (Jacobsen et al., 2004, Phillips et al., 1998).

The achievement gap is the product of multiple social and economic factors in society that place minority students at a disadvantage. There are factors within the social, political, and economic environment (e.g., lack of access to health care, adequate nutrition, and decent housing) and cultural clashes in society that frequently cause some students to disassociate with academics (Noguera, 2003). However, some students persevere despite these factors. While educators cannot influence all aspects of students' lives, this book is designed to help teachers develop pedagogies to close these achievement gaps and affirm diversity.

THE MULTIPLICITY AND INTERSECTIONALITY OF GAPS

In order to give full meaning to our discussion about eliminating the academic achievement gap, the conservation needs to be situated within a broader context—that of multiple gaps. Teachers and educational researchers argue that while the academic achievement gap helps to explain differences in students' performance in schools, it is only one of several gaps that challenge the academic success of students and the affirmation of diversity in U.S. society. Therefore, other gaps, such as the economic gap and health care gap, should also be considered during discussions about closing the academic achievement gap. These various gaps and their effects are interrelated and often serve to sustain one another.

Students who live on the downside of the gaps usually contend with multiple challenges. Being on the downside of a gap (e.g., health or economics) diminishes students' opportunities in other areas (e.g., school achievement) and magnifies the detrimental effects of outcome gaps (e.g., social mobility or career opportunity). Let us take the case of Leslie to illustrate how multiple gaps intersect. Leslie lives with her family in poverty and without health insurance. When she suffers from illness or injury, her poor health may go untreated because of a lack of health insurance and financial resources. The illness or injury may begin to interfere with, for example, her ability to eat, hear, concentrate, and sleep. As a consequence, her school performance may begin to slip. If the slip is not corrected—and here she will need the teacher's help—Leslie, a beautiful child with great potential, may fall into a pattern of low expectations and resign herself to this position. What is becoming increasingly clear is that students who excel in school must stay focused and on task.

EFFECTS OF THE ACADEMIC ACHIEVEMENT GAP

The academic achievement gap stands out more than the other gaps because academic achievements greatly influence the life chances of students. In addition, education in the United States has always been considered the great equalizer; for some, it is the cure-all for all social ills. That said, education does frequently (and increasingly) shape students' professional/career development, social mobility, self-esteem, and self-identity (Bandura, Barbaranelli, Caprara, & Pastorelli, 1996; Bandura, Barbaranelli, Vittorio, & Pastorelli, 2001). The academic achievement gap in reading, math, and science are especially noticeable between the rich and the poor, native speakers and nonnative speakers of English, and between White students and students of color. These gaps often reflect differences in social capital (e.g., access or connections between social networks) and power, because some groups have more benefits, as well as the clout to distribute them as they wish. To understand the causes and effects of the academic achievement gap, teachers need to examine how some groups exercise power over others in oppressive ways. For example, are some students in your classes behind in reading or math, not because they lack cognitive skills but because they, unlike their more socioeconomically privileged peers, have limited access to home computers with math games, personal tutors, or college-educated parents who know how to help them? In other words, they lack economic and social goods and resources—they lack social capital. See the following box for more information on poverty rates in America. Use the Reflection box as a way to apply the points made in the chapter to your own school situation.

1.1 Do You Know?

Poverty Rates

According to the U.S. Census Bureau (2007), the poverty rate in the U.S. for Blacks was 24.5 percent; Hispanics, 21.5 percent; Asians, 10.2 percent; and non-Hispanic Whites, 8.2 percent in 2004. Although the Midwest did not have the highest poverty rate among U.S. regions, it was the only region where the poverty rate increased from 2003 to 2007, from 10.7 to 11.1 percent.

1.1 Reflection

Can you find examples in your school of the intersection between different gaps (e.g., economic, health, legal treatment, and academic achievement gaps)?

Examples are

_____

_____

_____

How are these gaps related to racial issues?

_____

_____

_____

Describe one child for whom these gaps intersect.

_____

_____

_____

How are these gaps connected to that student's work in school?

_____

_____

_____

While such differences in opportunity may seem normal (simply "the way that it is") and out of the school's reach, such imbalances will only continue to grow in our competitive society unless we give students who are on the margins—through no fault of their own—solutions for tomorrow, the support and encouragement to catch up to their more socioeconomically privileged peers (e.g., opening honors and AP classes to students who are on the margins and strategically reaching out to them, counseling parents, holding accelerated summer institutes between middle and high school, and providing extra support such as afterschool computer clubs and mentors). That said, I know this is difficult because I hear from teachers, "Some of my students don't want to learn, so what am I suppose to do?" I take issue with this because I believe all students want to learn, even if they are very resistant to learning or to our teaching. It is our responsibility as teachers to reach our students and engage them in a way that makes learning meaningful to them.

Your first Action Plan follows and includes eight activities.

Action Plan 1: Revisiting the Struggle for Closing the Achievement Gap With Fresh Eyes

I. This week is the time to think back over your past experiences teaching children. If you are new to the teaching profession, consider your observations during student teaching situations. Often, standardized tests combined with the notion that "all children can succeed" give us the idea that children achieve in the same ways with the same results. Remember, students are not the same in the ways they learn or in the results they achieve. List several children who have not "achieved" according to your expectations. Describe their achievement behaviors and attitudes in your classroom as "case studies."

Students	Achievement Behavior	Attitude Toward Achieving
1.		
2.		
3.		

II. Analyze your beliefs about students labeled as "underachievers." For each of the numbered statements below, think of one or two ways of describing underachievers.

1. How would you describe underachievers?

_____

_____

2. Describe teaching challenges posed by this characteristic of underachievers.

_____

_____

3. Explain a teaching strategy to overcome this challenge.

_____

_____

4. Describe what underachievers are.

_____

_____

5. Describe teaching challenges posed by this characteristic of underachievers.

_____

_____

6. Explain a teaching strategy to overcome this challenge.

_____

_____

7. How would you describe underachievers?

_____

_____

8. Describe teaching challenges posed by this characteristic of underachievers.

_____

_____

9. Explain a teaching strategy to overcome this challenge.

_____

_____

III. What struggles are you having in your teaching because your beliefs about how and why students learn or don't learn are being challenged by information you are acquiring about the students, school policies, and the school climate?

(Continued)

(Continued)

Struggles with teaching

1. _____

2. _____

3. _____

IV. In what ways do you currently think about and reflect upon your students and your teaching?

Reflections on students

1. _____

2. _____

Reflections on teaching

1. _____

2. _____

V. How would you like to expand your reflections?

1. _____

2. _____

What barriers exist that hinder your reflections about students and teaching?

1. _____

2. _____

VI. List three examples from your teaching experience that show you are open to change, and three examples that show your resistance to change.

Open to change

1. _____

2. _____

3. _____

Resistance to change

1. _____

2. _____

3. _____

With a group or a partner, discuss what you see in one another's practice when you look at these lists?

_____

_____

What is your orientation to change?

_____

_____

_____

_____

VII. If you are open to challenging your prior way of thinking about students and your teaching, consider a child in your classroom who has been labeled as an "underachiever." Research the child in order to learn about that child's struggles and strengths. Explain reasons why this child may be struggling in school.

1.

_____

_____

2.

_____

_____

3.

_____

_____

(Continued)

Next, list strategies that will enhance the child's vision of value and achievement in school. If you need some ideas or resources to get you started, you might want to look at Theresa Perry's *Young, Gifted, and Black,* which describes ways to boost students' vision of themselves as high achievers.

1. My student's special interests and strengths include the following traits:

_____

_____

2. My student struggles with the following situations or subject areas:

_____

_____

3. Here are ways that I can increase my student's achievement and joy in school by drawing on the child's strengths and minimizing his or her struggles:

a.

_____

_____

b.

_____

_____

c.

_____

_____

d.

_____

_____

VIII. Commitment Statement (in your own handwriting)

Now, write a "commitment statement" to your future students. In it, describe a classroom in which all students will understand and appreciate their value as human beings and be able to achieve at a pace that is consistent with their ability. Commit yourself to exploring your students' experiences and backgrounds as well as their strengths in order to boost their identity formation and academic achievement. Don't worry if you don't have all of the answers as to how this will happen. That is what the rest of the weeks in this process are for. Think broadly, think big. Describe the ideal classroom for every child. Using your own handwriting to make this commitment to your future students is powerful. Even if you don't feel your ideas are very original or fully formed, use this as your starting point. You may even wish to share this with your current students and include them on this journey.

_____

_____

_____

_____

_____

Careful: Belief System Development in Progress

I firmly believe that all students can improve and grow in the traditional academic skills of reading (decoding and comprehension), writing with clarity and creativity, and math reasoning skills. However, knowing that not all students learn in the same way or have the same interests can lead us as teachers to valuable discoveries about our students' strengths in areas of more nontraditionally acknowledged talents. Consider the multiple intelligences of Howard Gardner (1993) as a way to begin:

- Linguistic intelligence ("word smart")
- Logical-mathematical intelligence ("number/reasoning smart")
- Spatial intelligence ("picture smart")
- Bodily-kinesthetic intelligence ("body smart")
- Musical intelligence ("music smart")
- Interpersonal intelligence ("people smart")
- Intrapersonal intelligence ("self smart")
- Naturalist intelligence ("nature smart")
  1. List names of your students next to each of the intelligences. Where do their strengths shine through?
  2. Plan at least one way to bring each form of intelligence into some learning experience in your classroom this week. For example, you

(Continued)

could have students with an "interpersonal intelligence" lead study sessions with small groups of their classmates, where they design a "review session" for a subject area. You will discover many natural "teachers" in this way!

This, I Believe

_____

_____

_____

Post these statements, along with your additions to them, in a prominent place in your plan book or on your desk.

1. My students do not misbehave or "underachieve" in order to torture me. They are here to find their way in the world and they need me to believe in them.

2. My students are ALL valuable and excellent. They all have gifts and strengths. Some gifts and strengths may be hidden or affected by past experiences in school. The students need me to illuminate their gifts and strengths during instructional time.

3. All of my students can achieve academically. It is my job as their teacher to make sure this happens.

4. My students are resilient. They can overcome challenging circumstances with encouragement and opportunity. I must find a way to see that they have the opportunity to do so. What I will do includes the following ideas:

_____

_____

2 Diversity and Power

Hanushek and his colleagues (2008) ask, "Is it a few rocket scientists at the very top of the distribution who spur economic growth, or is it 'education for all' that is needed? The answer, is not one or the other but both" (p. 2). Their question and response highlight the significance of teachers making certain that all students learn. In this chapter, I address diversity and its relationship to achievement and discuss the influence of unequal power relations.

DIVERSITY

When did you *really* begin to notice a steady increase in diversity? In the places where you frequently go? Perhaps you noticed it during a trip to the shopping mall or during lunch or dinner at a restaurant? Maybe you acknowledged the increase in diversity in the student population at your school when someone made a comment that children from several migrant families or refugees from Somalia had enrolled. Or perhaps it was when your principal announced that the school would start a bilingual or English as a second language (ESL) program or when you saw a statistic that reported 50% of your students were eligible for free and reduced lunches. On the other hand, maybe you began to notice diversity because of its absence. In other words, you noticed it at the mall or restaurant but not in your school. Ironically, in your school you noticed that things were becoming less racially and ethnically diverse and that there was silence surrounding the diversity that is taking place in the larger society and the absence of that diversity in your school. Here you might be reminded of Orfield and Yun (1999) and Boger and Orfield (2005) who contend that, in some urban areas and in some places in the South, there is a trend toward the racial and socioeconomic resegregation of schools.

2.1 Reflection

Can you recall your first experiences with diverse students in your classroom or school (e.g., the first time your students' race, ethnicity, and/or native language differed from your own or the first time you were assigned to teach a class where students of color outnumbered White students or equaled almost one-third to one-half of the students)?

Describe your first experience with diverse students.

_____

_____

_____

How did you acknowledge this change?

_____

_____

_____

2.2 Reflection

What is your definition of diversity? Compare your definition with a teacher/friend. Next, the two of you should compare your definitions with the statement on diversity below. But first, list your definitions and discuss their similarities and differences. How do they compare and contrast?

The following is my definition of diversity.

_____

_____

_____

The similarities and differences with a teacher/friend are listed below.

Similarities

_____

_____

_____

Differences

_____

_____

_____

My definition of diversity involves the intersections of race, ethnicity, gender identity, disability, social class, language, sexual orientation, and religion, as they operate in school policies and practices, as well as in the larger society. In other words, a person has multiple positions, roles, and identities that interact in different ways in different settings with their social markers of gender, social status, ethnicity/race, and sexual orientation. Language and religion/spirituality are also social markers that influence a person's positions, roles, and identities. The discussion of diversity presented here focuses on individual/personal experiences in the school context; however, keep in mind that this discussion is taking place within the current local and global context. Further, the diversity of knowledge, life histories, and contexts described here is central to efforts aimed at challenging the status quo.

2.3 Reflection

How do you identify and describe your social markers (e.g., ethnicity, social class)?

Provide a description of your social markers.

_____

_____

_____

2.4 Reflection

What do you think about my definition of diversity?

_____

_____

_____

How does it compare with the definitions of you and your teacher/friends?

_____

_____

_____

What can I learn from you and what can you learn from my definition? When we have a cup of coffee together, what will you say to me about my definition? Give me your best shot; I can take it!

_____

_____

_____

AFFIRMING DIVERSITY

Throughout this publication, I not only discuss diversity but I discuss affirming diversity. By affirming diversity, I mean teachers taking a deliberate and active stance to support the histories, cultures, and equitable inclusion in schools and society of different sociocultural groups. Affirming diversity includes teachers working to correct biased and stereotypical thinking; teaching in ways that include multiple perspectives, narratives, and ways of understanding; and addressing issues of power and privilege so that all students may be successful.

Diversity in its multiple forms is an observable fact of life today. However, diversity without real engagement is simply a hollow phrase (Eck, 1997). In other words, supporting diversity requires understanding, accepting, and appreciating ourselves, our colleagues, our students, and their families. This affirmation of diversity has several benefits for teachers, including increased collegiality among faculty and greater understanding of students, subject areas, and resources that are essential to a strong professional learning community. Diversity inspires innovation as both teachers and students have opportunities to complete these activities:

- Engage in cross-cultural relationships
- Observe various combinations of learning and teaching styles
- Develop linguistic proficiency in more than one language

A comment I often hear from teachers across the United States is that they appreciate "diversity" because it makes teaching more exciting! It both interrupts what is boring and plays a crucial role in overcoming gaps that are harmful to students and teachers alike.

If we return to the example of Leslie, we can see how varied one's experiences may be despite similar circumstances. If you will recall, Leslie lives in poverty. The social differences between other students and Leslie, as well as between teachers and Leslie, may include varied levels of consciousness, opportunities, and cultural perspectives. These differences may result in a range of experiences that may be both similar to and different from those of students and teachers with very different histories than Leslie. The varied experiences may relate to any of the following circumstances:

- Students' and teachers' regional or national mobility
- Changes in family composition
- Differential treatment in schools and other social institutions based on, for example, class, race, and/or language differences
- Knowledge of personal history and ancestry
- Personal experience with a cognitive and/or physical disability
- The kind of employment sought for the acquisition of income

To affirm students' diversity means to acknowledge, accept, and contextualize their cultural history, background, and experiences in your teaching. Such affirmation requires identifying the particular knowledge, skills, and dispositions that you bring to the classroom and determining areas in which you still need to grow. Let me share a short story on this point.

I clearly remember my first opportunity to affirm ethnic and racial diversity in the classroom as a teacher. The opportunity occurred when I was substituting in Chicago. One morning, I received a call from the Sub Center to report to a school on the far northwest side of Chicago. I wondered why I was being sent to a school so far away; perhaps more puzzling to me was that I was requested to report to an all-White school. During my substitute experience and those of my Black substitute friends, we were rarely asked to substitute in a school on the far north side during the 1960s and 1970s. I did not hesitate or have second thoughts about going to the school, in part because I was curious to see a White school—plus, I had new car payments to make and was just happy to be working!

My initial arrival at the school raised a few eyebrows, but I was greeted cordially and professionally and escorted to a biology classroom that remained my room for the next two weeks. The biology teacher I was substituting for had to deal with an emergency that required him to leave the country for two weeks. During the first few days of my substituting, I noticed distinct grouping patterns (where they sat, how they interacted) among the Irish, Italian, and Polish students. There was tension—not a great deal, but some—between these groups of students. The knowledge base for my insights came from my experiences in the Army and having had the opportunity to live, work, and socialize with soldiers from many ethnic backgrounds.

Realizing this tension, and taking advantage of my "celebrity" status, which came from the students' curiosity about me because they had never had a Black teacher—plus, I really knew my subject matter and how to teach it—I began to discuss with them how scientists of different ethnic groups, including women, had worked together and drawn upon the work of one another to come up with many of the things (e.g., products) that make living easier for all of us. The students were surprised that such cross-cultural relations existed. I shared with them a few stories from my army experience that included members of different ethnic groups working together and helping one another. They stated that no one had ever talked to them before about how different ethnic groups have worked together, especially the Irish, Italian, and Polish. Also, they wanted to know how I knew so much about these cross-cultural relationships. My response was a smile, along with, "You, too, can see these groups working together if you watch a Notre Dame, Chicago Bears, University of Illinois, or Northwestern football game this weekend. Cut out the roster of players from the newspaper so you will know who is who and just watch how well they get along with one another."

2.5 Reflection

Have you noticed that dealing with the achievement gap and diversity is both intrapersonal and multidirectional?

The intrapersonal aspect involves how one sees oneself or thinks about the world based upon one's own experiences. Individuals have their own set of positive and negative experiences with diversity, and students have a set of experiences that affect their classroom attitude.

Discuss your positive experiences with diversity.

_____

_____

_____

Discuss your negative experiences with diversity.

_____

_____

_____

Explain your neutral or colorblind experiences with diversity.

_____

_____

_____

The multidirectional aspect involves the relationships between and among groups throughout history, as well as how the memories of those experiences play out in and beyond the classroom.

Write a short reaction to the following questions and discuss them with a teacher/friend.

How can different historical and cultural experiences cause miscommunication in a classroom and, as a result, further widen achievement gaps?

_____

_____

_____

How do both of these ideas (intrapersonal and multidirectional) relate to teacher-student and student-student interactions in your classroom? For example, some students of color may question the fairness of White teachers based on their previous experiences with some White people. Or some middle-class African American teachers

(Continued)

(Continued)

> may doubt the resiliency of poor African American students. What
> examples do you have from your classroom work?
>
> _____
>
> _____
>
> _____

ALL TEACHERS NEED TO LEARN ABOUT DIVERSITY

Let me be clear that I am talking to all teachers at all grade levels. Often, when discussing "diversity," many teachers of color argue that they understand "diversity" because they are the Other (e.g., marginalized, silenced, and invisible). Teachers of color are often the Other so I have very little argument with this point. However, being the Other doesn't necessarily mean that a teacher will automatically foster a pluralistic classroom. In addition, African American teachers have much to learn about teaching Latino students. Similarly, Chinese American teachers have much to learn about teaching Hmong students who have recently come from Southeast Asia. This learning about diversity is much more than simply learning facts and histories about other cultures and groups. It includes learning how to teach in a way that helps each student to learn the knowledge and skills and developing the disposition that helps them achieve a thriving and fulfilling life both inside and outside the bounds of the economy.

In addition, in the "flat world" about which Thomas Friedman (2006) writes, instances of having to deal with diversity are increasing. Interactions with people from China, India, and other countries are growing. Our global society will thus require that no single group of Americans have an advantage over other groups simply because of who they are rather than what they have accomplished. Everyone must examine their knowledge of diversity and, based upon that examination, strengthen their understanding of difference and alter discriminatory or biased actions.

Consequently, diversifying the racial/ethnic composition of the teaching force so that it reflects the racial/ethnic composition of students is necessary. Teachers of color are often more than role models. They are cultural translators, brokers, and advocates for culturally diverse groups of students, thereby contributing directly to the students' school achievement (Carter, 2005; Dilworth & Brown, 2008; Fultz, 1995; Gay, 1993; Irvine, 2001).

POWER IN THE CONTEXT OF CHANGE

Power is not often explicitly addressed when discussing change/transition in schools. However, recognizing the presence of power in relationships and the school contexts is crucial to developing appropriate, effective strategies for eliminating the achievement gap. Understanding power relations in the harder work to make schools more effective in dealing with the achievement gap and the challenges to bring about good public education is essential. In some schools that I visit, some teachers' way of dealing with power is through empowering their less-privileged students by celebrating differences. Attention to difference alone, however, does not guarantee that students will become empowered.

What is the power dynamic between you and your students and between you and the building-level and district-level administration? Many teachers I work with argue that they are simply too busy to examine the nature and function of power relations in their classrooms, schools, and districts. Are you one of those teachers, or do you and your teacher friends "speak truth to power"? In other words, do you speak up when equity and/or equality concerns for any of your students are about to be ignored or overlooked? Do you make your views about the challenges to public education known to elected officials and power brokers?

Power circulates among the people working in schools and society and is not only found in top-down relations (e.g., federal government to state, state to school superintendent, school superintendent to principal, principal to teachers, teachers to students). Power relations are more complicated than an oppressor/oppressed model suggests. Power exists and circulates between people in all relationships, and power relations are constantly changing (Foucault, 1977).

To advocate for equality in power relations, discussions about *student empowerment*, *agency* (e.g., teachers and students as agents of change), and *advocacy* (e.g., parents and teachers as advocates of children) should take place. Understanding the scope of these terms/concepts is important to closing achievement gaps and affirming diversity. Additionally, educators must recognize the power they possess if they are not to "abuse it or fail to maximize it for their students' benefit" (Cooper, 2003, p. 104).

Power goes beyond teachers' ability to bring in more multicultural history and perspectives. Although a good start, just bringing in history is not enough. Teachers need to use history to point to and critique ideas and practices that positively and negatively influence the life circumstances of different groups of people over time. Let me comment here. It is academically and socially beneficial for students to learn about positive developments in society that particularly relate to them. Sometimes there is too much gloom and doom, where all seems to be bad in the area where they live. African American or Latino students should be encouraged to see that there is progress. However, don't get uptight if they dis your comment; they still hear you and your power as a teacher is in high gear. Similarly, please don't take for granted that the girls are doing fine; short conversations before and after class can help with their self-actualization, and recommending a book or having them work on something special where it is just you and them is a powerful way to personally help students and for them to appreciate the teacher-student dynamic. Now, back to business!

Bringing more multicultural information to class illustrates only one facet of the power teachers have. Even if teachers are told which textbook topics to teach, their knowledge of the perspectives that the textbook includes and omits is critical to the knowledge development of their students. Additionally, teachers have the power to decide how to address students' perceived shortcomings. A teacher can choose supportive, negative, or bland statements to discuss a student's work, and these choices, along with the teacher's overall attitude toward a student, can affect personal identity and/or group identity formation. Furthermore, the teacher has the power to decide whether to persevere or give up when trying to reach students who struggle. The list goes on and on: Teachers exercise power affecting students' lives with every choice that they make in the classroom. In most discussions of school improvement, power is not explicitly addressed. However, power relations affect all aspects of the educational landscape, including which textbooks are adopted, how schools are organized, who gets hired and fired, and what agenda items appear on Parent Teacher Organization (PTO) meeting agendas. Therefore, recognizing how power is exercised among various people and in different contexts is crucial to understanding which strategies can best close the achievement gap and affirm diversity. Lisa Delpit (1996) offers a helpful story from the Athabaskan culture in Alaska to reinforce the importance of considering unequal power relations between teachers and students in the classrooms.

A little boy went out with his grandfather and other men to hunt bear. After capturing a bear and placing it in a pit for skinning, the grandfather sent the boy for water to assist in the process. As the boy moved away from the group, his grandfather called after him, "Run, run, the bear is after you!" The boy tensed, started to run, then stopped and calmly continued walking. His grandfather called again, louder, "Run, run I say! This bear is going to catch and eat you!" But the boy continued to walk. When the boy returned with the water, his grandfather was very happy. He had passed the test.

The test the boy passed was to disregard the words of another, even those of a knowledgeable and trusted grandfather, if the information presented conflicted with his own perceptions. When children who have been brought up to trust their own observations enter school, they confront teachers, who, in their estimation, act as unbelievable tyrants. From the children's perspective, their teachers attempt to coerce behavior, even in such completely personal decisions as when to go to the bathroom or when to get a drink of water. The bell rings, go to lunch; the lights blink, put your work away, whether you are finished or not. Despite the rhetoric of American education, it does not teach children to be independent, but rather to be dependent on external sources for direction, for truth, for meaning. It trains children both to seek meaning solely from the text and to seek truth outside of their own good sense—concepts that are foreign and dangerous to Alaskan village communities. (pp. 101–102)

Delpit's illustration shows how teachers may perceive a student as defiant when the student has no such intention of acting defiantly. The student's upbringing and cultural values are different than the teacher's. Without better cultural understandings between the teacher and student, miscommunication is likely to occur, and the teacher may unwittingly exercise power to get students to conform, thinking that this is in the students' best interest. A wiser use of power would be one that facilitates both the teacher's and students' learning about each others' cultural values. In order to best teach students and close achievement gaps, a teacher with a culture different from that of the students should continually pursue an understanding of the students' cultures.

2.6 Reflection

Discuss with two teacher/friends where you see the exercise of "power" within your school:

- Examine how other staff members are exercising power in school relationships.
- Examine how you are exercising power in your interactions with others at school.
- Examine how these power relationships work, whom they serve, and the effects they produce.

(Continued)

(Continued)

How do you envision the power relationships within the school contributing to or hindering closure of the achievement gap?

_____

_____

_____

WHERE IS POWER IN YOUR SCHOOL?

Liu and Pope-Davis's (2003) observations about power help us see the connections between the affirmation of diversity, multiculturalism, and power. Their diagram also helps us understand why and how power relations should be recognized and actions taken to diversify school policies and procedures. Liu and Pope-Davis contend that change/transition in schools will only meet with resistance and failure when power is unrecognized or mapped only within a particular environment. I borrow (and modify somewhat) Liu and Pope-Davis's illustration of how actions to diversify education interact with a recognition or lack of recognition of power (see Figure 2.1).

Figure 2.1

	Power	
	Unrecognized	*Recognized*
Action to Diversify	Status quo 1	Relativism 2
	Superficial diversity 3	Multicultural education/ multiculturalism 4

In other words, Cell 1 shows the status quo. As Liu and Pope-Davis (2003) argue, "In this environment, multiculturalism and diversity are not regarded as important, resources are not concentrated toward understanding the importance of diversifying, and the traditional power structures are left intact and in place" (p. 98). This dynamic is likely to occur in a school where miscommunications between school personnel and students are seen as the fault of the students and their families. For example, teachers may view students whose primary language is not English as not trying hard enough to bridge the achievements gap. Additionally, teachers may perceive a lack of effort on the part of the student's family to learn English as resistance to the American way of life. Under such circumstances, whether the teachers' perceptions are true or not, power relations between the school and home will most likely remain intact because teachers see the students' home culture as a weakness.

In the second cell, when power is recognized but there is no concerted action to diversify, the result is relativism.

> *Relativism is the belief that virtually anything and everything is tolerable and acceptable because if a culture values it and sanctions it, then "we" must also recognize its inherent value to that culture. . . . Power is recognized as an important variable to contend with, but rather than engaging in the struggle, the preference is to stagnate in the discourse over power. Consequently, the belief for people in this environment is that everything is valuable and salient and that we should not have to struggle to determine what this all means for us. (Liu & Pope-Davis, 2003, p. 98)*

Relativism may be seen in schools where staff members bring up the difference between the culture of some families and the school. The staff may even recognize and discuss how society economically marginalizes some families, resulting in the need for some students to work or, as noted in our example below, participate in the family business before they are old enough to legally do so. However, rather than confront the conflict between working and studying and its relationship to the society's larger economy, the staff may attribute the decision to work as an aspect of the families' racial and/or ethnic culture—or as evidence that the family "doesn't care" about education. Despite their inaction, school staff members in this situation may view themselves as "multicultural." Let me note here that discussions that come out of Cell 2 are a bit tricky; for example, speaking English, being White, male, and heterosexual are not extended to new arrivals (e.g., Hmong). Such (in)actions then lead to (in this example) the Hmong adopting the customs such as generations living together and working together in a business in order to be successful in their new life circumstance.

In the third cell, as people move to diversify but do not recognize power, the result will invariably be a "diverse" community that stands on a troubled foundation (Liu & Pope-Davis, 2003). This "superficial diversity" occurs when the school staff has not identified, critiqued, and reconceptualized old frameworks and structures. Examples of superficial diversity in a school might include a Black history program or a Cinco de Mayo celebration, as well as collections of "multicultural" materials in the classroom. Although these examples are not inherently superficial, they become so when they are implemented without attention to how inequities based on race, class, and ability operate in a school's hidden curriculum. Additionally, criteria outlined for a "highly qualified teacher" that do not include culturally responsive pedagogy will not result in the closure of achievement gaps. Simply put, the introduction of diverse elements will not lead to substantial and comprehensive transformation in schools when power remains unrecognized. However, if the perspectives of marginalized and historically oppressed cultures are not introduced as a regular part of history, and students and staff do not understand the social, economic, and political effects of marginalizing these perspectives, then students (both White middle-class students and "others") will not become empowered to work for change in their own lives and the lives of others.

The fourth cell represents the achievement of multiculturalism; power is recognized and people move toward diversification. Here, the affirmation of diversity means recognizing how power functions in all training, activities, and actions. In other words, power becomes the unconscious schema by which we organize and make sense of our environments (Liu & Pope-Davis, 2003, p. 98). A school located in this cell will recognize how and why society favors certain groups of people by giving them access to disproportionate amounts of resources and power. The school will actively work to give all students access to opportunities through both accelerated academic achievement and an examination and inclusion of culturally relevant practices. Additionally, staff will examine the school's "hidden curriculum," or the curriculum that is not written down in any textbook or lesson plan but that is conveyed to students and their families via staff words, attitudes, and actions. For example, the hidden curriculum may include an association between individual laziness and poverty. This curriculum is subtle but powerful. In a split second, a teacher can send the message that students are unacceptable as they currently are.

Adhering to Cell 4 will eliminate achievement gaps and affirm diversity via new relationships and the transformation of old ones. This work is ongoing and challenging, as new issues will continuously emerge and colleagues will disagree over the ways and means to effect positive change. A deeper understanding of how power operates within school walls will not make unequal power relations between colleagues disappear. However, identifying and talking about how power functions in our own backyard are essential to helping students achieve academic success.

Power and Agency

John Thompson's (1984) description of power may be useful to your understanding of power.

> *A satisfactory analysis of the phenomenon of power requires a detailed account of the relations between action, institutions and social structure, since each of these levels realizes an aspect of power. At the level of action and in the most general sense, "power" is the ability to act in pursuit of one's aims and interest: an agent has* the power to act, *the power to intervene in the sequence of events and to alter their course. At the institutional level, "power" is a capacity which* enables or empowers *some agents to make decisions, pursue ends or realize interests. Finally, as an institutionally endowed capacity, power is* limited *by social structure, that is, by the structural conditions which circumscribe the range of institutional variation.* (p. 28, emphasis original)

2.7 Reflection

Review the above section on power with a teacher/friend and discuss the different ways you see imbalances in the exercise of power between these groups:

- The rich and poor
- Native and nonnative English speakers
- White students and students of color
- Students who are gay and students who are straight

Can you identify other disparities between social groups that limit students' academic achievement?

_____

_____

_____

(Continued)

(Continued)

Analyze Liu and Pope-Davis's (2003) diagram in Figure 2.1:

In which cell is your school?

_____

Do staff members in your school recognize power relations and undertake actions to affirm diversity?

_____

Give examples that support your cell choice.

_____

2.1 Take Action

Identify an inequity that you have tolerated so as not to "rock the boat." Take action to bring about change.

_____

Going forward with my action of change when faced with this inequity might include

_____

What are the risks or consequences for taking this action?

_____

Action Plan 2: Affirming Diversity in Your Classroom and Power Structures in Society

I. There are many different ways to affirm diversity in your classroom. This week take another step in this direction. Consider, for example, researching your students' ethnic background. Begin by listing the different ethnic groups you know about in your classroom:

1.

_____

2.

_____

3.

_____

4.

_____

5.

_____

II. Design a classroom lesson that encourages students to share the history of their ethnic groups with pride. Remind students that saying, "I am just an American" leaves out or denies the history of their grandparents and refutes the observation that all Americans, with the exception of Native Americans, came from another country or place. Also, keep in mind that when a White American declares that "I am just an American"—while labeling people of color as African Americans, Latinos, or Asian Americans—this is yet another way to make the White experience the norm, to reinforce White privilege, and to construct people of color as *Others* and outsiders. Additionally, think of the next steps you will take to include a variety of cultural experiences and perspectives in your classroom.

(Continued)

(Continued)

III. Over the weekend, pay close attention to power structures in society and school. Remember that as a person from a dominant group (e.g., heterosexual, upper class, nondisabled), as a person who is educated, and/or as a middle-class professional, your own experiences of power are often hidden. If you are having trouble identifying your power advantages and privileges, partner with a friend from a different cultural group, either a teacher/friend or other friend. Go on an "apartment hunt" together as an experiment. Compare your experiences. Go shopping together at a jewelry store or open-air market. Notice if there are small reactions from shopkeepers related to perceived aspects of identity.

IV. Consider the effect the power structure has on your students who live on the "downside" of the power structures in society. They will often need to use a "double consciousness," Du Bois (1994)—meaning that, while they strongly believe in themselves and their abilities, they will need to be aware of how they are perceived by those who own and/or control major institutions or by the gatekeepers from whom they seek opportunities or services. This push and pull of ideas about self can have a dehumanizing result and can cause a feeling of anxiety and frustration that most people in privileged positions will not experience on a regular basis.

Consider the child you described in Action Plan 1 (or choose another child). How do power structures in society play out in this child's life, both in and out of school?

Power structures in society influence (name of student)'s life in the following ways:

_____

_____

V. How can you counteract unequal power relations in your classroom? Consider how unequal power structures are a barrier to students' achievement and life chances. Think of ways that you can bring sociopolitical consciousness to all of your students as you bolster each student's agency and self-esteem. Gloria Ladson-Billings's (1995) theory of culturally relevant pedagogy may be a helpful guide here. Her theory has three tenets: academic achievement, cultural competence (in both one's own and the dominant culture), and teaching students to be critical of the dominant social order.

Also consider how your own sociopolitical consciousness affects students' achievement and life chances. In addition, consider the connections between personal empowerment and a rich and thriving life both within and outside of economy.

I will raise the sociopolitical consciousness of my students by completing the following actions: (Remember Ladson-Billings's three tenets.)

1.

_____

2.

_____

3.

_____

VI. What leadership roles or roles of responsibility can you give to the child in the classroom? I am going to give the following students the specific leadership roles or roles of responsibility in the classroom: Remember, give students responsibility that will require them to develop this behavior. Being the lunch counter or line leader is minimal responsibility; push for and demand much more.

_____

_____

_____

_____

3 Becoming Socially Critical and Fostering a Caring Community

I n the previous chapters, I discussed the achievement gaps, power, and how to raise students' achievement levels by affirming diversity in the schools. In this chapter, I address caring with a sociopolitical consciousness, becoming socially critical, and fostering a caring community among students. I begin with caring with sociopolitical consciousness.

CARING WITH SOCIOPOLITICAL CONSCIOUSNESS

Parents want teachers who care for their children—that is, teachers whose actions demonstrate more than ministerial caring (e.g., sending a child to the school's nurse or repeating the directions for a lesson). While there are numerous ways to enact caring, I suggest the fusion of the idea of caring with the idea of consciousness or caring with sociopolitical consciousness (e.g., Noddings, 1995).

Caring with sociopolitical consciousness involves awareness and understanding of how student groups have fared historically in schools and it involves understanding how current social factors perpetuate barriers to the scholastic advancement of some students and not others. Teachers who care with a sociopolitical consciousness know the research on how students are treated in schools as a result of ability group tracking, zero tolerance policies, budget reduction in per pupil expenditures, and referrals to special education. In addition, teachers who care with sociopolitical consciousness really get to know their students. Here, I am speaking about "getting to know" in a much more authentic sense than knowledge about students which comes from surveys, sociometric inventories, school records, and/or short discussions about a student's interests. These notions of getting to know students may be unconsciously guided by "color-blind" treatment, or treating everyone equally. In Catherine Cornbleth's (2008) book, *Diversity and the New Teacher,* she writes really powerfully about how color-blind teaching is incompatible with culturally relevant teaching; how color-blindness is actually blindness to white privilege. She asks of color blindness, "When we don't 'see' race or don't think it matters, what assumptions are we making? How might race and racism affect teaching? Learning? How might treating 'all students the same' be unfair, advantaging some students and disadvantaging others? What forms of individualism am I using? In what ways do they engage students' interests and promote their talents? How do they foster conformity and assimilation to middle-class, White, or other norms and standards?" (p. 89). And Jacqueline I. Irvine (2001) in *Educating Teachers for Diversity: Seeing With a Cultural Eye,* writes, "Many teachers erroneously believe that if they recognize the race of their students or discuss issues of ethnicity in their classroom, they might be labeled as insensitive or, worse, racist. However, when teachers ignore their students' ethnic identities and their unique cultural beliefs, perceptions, values, and worldviews, they fail as culturally responsive pedagogists. Color-blind teachers claim that they treat all students 'the same,' which usually means that all students are treated as if they are, or should be, both White and middle class" (p. xvii).

Caring about students as individuals, of course, is a positive way of caring. Nevertheless, it tends to be more ministerial and is not caring with a sociopolitical consciousness, which always takes into account students' social context and group identities. Further (and this comment is a bit tricky), caring with a sociopolitical consciousness does not mean arguing or stating how you deeply care for students and that you understand their sociopolitical context, but then, almost within the same breath, you denigrate the students' parents and community as not caring about their children's education. Thus, you see yourself as having to "make up for" what the students are not getting at home.

Caring with sociopolitical consciousness may also be illustrated by a teacher who cares for a student named Jonah and his ability to demonstrate his math literacy. However, if the teacher calls on Jonah, Jeff, and Jack without calling on Julia, he or she may be neglecting the larger social context that presents males as leaders in math and science advancement while ignoring how females are marginalized in these fields, a point I referenced above. Caring with a sociopolitical consciousness leads to the acknowledgement of how certain knowledge and skills are privileged by the dominant society and used by those in power to keep barriers in place. In turn, teachers can use this knowledge about power to more carefully guide students toward achievement.

Teachers can accomplish "caring" in different ways. Therefore, it is up to them to work out their caring platforms or philosophies. The following example may be useful. Irvine (2001) tells us about two caring and competent teachers found in Miles Corwin's *And Still We Rise: The Trial and Triumphs of 12 Gifted Inner-City High School Students.*

> *Corwin's story is about two veteran, caring, and competent English teachers, who work in an urban school mainly populated by African American students. One teacher, Ms. Little, is White and has a strong political consciousness and believes her students' race and family income are irrelevant to her work as a teacher. The other teacher, Ms. Moultrie, is an African American, and the students call her Mama Moultrie. Ms. Little believes that her mission is to help students pass the English AP exam so that they can succeed in college and leave the hardship of the community where they live. Ms. Moultrie's actions are those of a parent surrogate, and her classroom is an environment where she uses literature to teach values, racial pride and uplift, and hard work. Ms. Little believes that Ms. Moultrie talks too much about race and social inequities and too little about essay structure and thesis development. She does not see herself in a parental role. "I'm not their damn mama," Little says, "I am their English teacher." Ms. Moultrie answers Ms. Little's criticism that she spends too little time teaching content and too much time preaching by claiming that she is preparing black students not merely for college but for life. (p. 4)*

Irvine (2001) writes, "These two caring and competent teachers are so different in their philosophy about their personal and professional roles as teachers, their mission and efficacy, their practice and beliefs, their students, and the communities in which they work" (p. 6). And once again, they both care.

3.1 Reflection

Reflect on the caring of Ms. Little and Ms. Moultrie:
Which teacher do you think more exhibits a sense or caring with a sociopolitical consciousness?

_____

Which teacher is more closely aligned with your own views?

_____

In what ways?

_____

_____

Why does each teacher believe what she believes?

_____

_____

What are the benefits and limitations of the approaches of each teacher?

_____

_____

What particular things do you do to demonstrate caring for your students?

_____

_____

Teachers have to care for students in ways that matter to those students as individuals and as members of social groups. The ability to care with a sociopolitical consciousness comes through knowing students as people whose roles are numerous (e.g., sibling, son/daughter, teammate, volunteer).

Recently, a high school teacher, Bee, told me about the difficulty she was having with a student who had just arrived from México. The student's home responsibilities in México were consistent with those of an adult. For example, he had a full-time job and sometimes cared for younger siblings while his parents worked. The student was having a difficult time adjusting to being treated like a young adolescent at school when at home he held what many people in the United States consider to be adult responsibilities. Bee went on to say that once she discovered the source of the tension, she and the student were able to work out a solution that both respected school and classroom rules and honored the student's personal cultural integrity.

Teachers engaged in caring with a sociopolitical consciousness are certain and definitive in their action. They teach from the position of being intolerant about the lack of progress some groups have made and continue to make in the education system—or as Paolo Freire describes, they teach with an "impatient patience" (Freire, 1970/2007). To this end, their teaching takes into account the barriers that students of color and other marginalized groups face, and they therefore always go about their teaching in a way that speaks truth to power, that challenges inequality in education policies and practices, and that teaches students the literacies of freedom, citizenship, and social justice.

BECOMING SOCIALLY CRITICAL

When teachers care with sociopolitical consciousness for students, they feel concern about the social barriers that adversely affect the students and the cultural groups to which they belong. In order to stay up-to-date about the current social issues affecting students and teachers alike, teachers may wish to read community newspapers and take advantage of the Internet. When using the Internet, I suggest typing particular keywords into a search engine like Google or Yahoo. The keywords should include the subject (e.g., reading, math) and the issue (e.g., gender inequality). Don't feel overwhelmed when many citations for articles, books, and reports come up—OK, be overwhelmed a little! However, I have never been disappointed after selectively reviewing the search results. I always retrieve material that is informative and that strengthens my ability to analyze social issues regarding students. In addition, I can refer my students to the fruits of my labor so that they may also investigate the issue and become more socially aware. As Ladson-Billings (1994) states, "Not only must teachers encourage academic success and cultural competence; they must help students recognize, understand, and critique current social inequities" (p. 22). This is critical for teaching students how to critique social inequities; how to be fluent in the literacies of freedom, citizenship, and social justice as represented in the U.S. Constitution, Bill of Rights, and other foundational American documents; and how to use these documents and liberties to serve their human and civil rights concerns. Examples of this kind of teaching with a socially critical consciousness can be found in the publications, *Rethinking Schools* and *Teaching Tolerance*—periodicals written by and for teachers on teaching for social change.

FOSTERING A CARING COMMUNITY AMONG STUDENTS

Not only should teachers care for their students, but students should also care for each other, as well as people in the larger community. Fostering a sociopolitically caring community among students promotes a community of learners who are able to effect change in the world. Instead of focusing on competition or materialism ("I'm smarter than you," "I did better on the test than you," "I have more baseball cards than you," and so forth), students who care with a sociopolitical consciousness understand how being part of a community, whether local or global, means reaching out to others. Such reaching out and helping one another might include helping a homework buddy, working with younger students as a "reading buddy," assisting each other in group activities, and structuring additional activities that help students give to others rather than focusing only on themselves. Fostering a caring community, I have learned from most teachers, begins when students first arrive at a school and/or the teachers send out a note before the beginning of the semester introducing themselves to students and parents, welcoming them to the school and classroom. From there, fostering a caring, learning community includes the development of a learning vision, curriculum goals, and values in collaboration with the students in a supportive, risk-taking environment that promotes inquiry. Also included in caring communities are the collective establishment of "solutions for tomorrow"—classroom management and self-discipline rules, regulations, and spirit that offer accountability toward, for example, students working cooperatively; receiving support and opportunity to showcase their gifts and talents; listening when someone is talking; asking if they can help if someone doesn't understand; being a good friend and classmate.

Action Plan 3: Caring With Sociopolitical Consciousness

During this week, I encourage you to continue on the journey you have begun. You have had a taste of what affirming diversity and addressing power relations can do to close achievement gaps. Continue to expand your own horizons as you teach. Design a strategy to bring each of the following culturally relevant practices into your classroom:

1. A teacher/student relationship that is fluid, respectful, affirming, and extends to interactions beyond the classroom and into the community

_____

_____

_____

_____

2. Connectedness with all students

_____

_____

_____

_____

3. Incentives to encourage a "community of learners"

_____

_____

_____

_____

4. Incentives to encourage students to learn collaboratively as they teach each other and become responsible for each other

_____

_____

_____

_____

Part II

The Change Process

Consider the following statement:

> The very things we now wish that we could hold onto and keep safe from change were themselves originally produced by change. (Bridges, 2003, p. 5)

This statement implicitly argues that the change process involves the individual, the teacher, and the organization—in other words, the school. As noted previously, the journey toward closing achievement gaps and affirming diversity is complex, nonlinear, and filled with uncertainties and excitement. Changes challenge the relationship between and among teacher/friends and demand vision, planning, benchmarks, and attention to the operation of power relations at the individual and organizational level.

II.1 Reflection

Close your eyes and imagine your ideal classroom. What do you see?

____

____

(Continued)

(Continued)

Whom do you see?

_____

_____

What do you see as ideal in your present classroom?

_____

_____

What do you need to do to move your present classroom closer to your ideal?

_____

_____

II.2 Reflection

Reflect on the changes you want to see in your school. What changes in school policies, practices, beliefs, and attitudes are most critical to closing achievement gaps?

_____

_____

_____

What is your role in catalyzing this change? How can your school and central administration provide the leadership and support needed to make these changes a reality?

_____

_____

_____

II.1 Take Action

Think about a struggling student in your class or school. How have societal structures, cultural contexts, and the student's individual agency (choices, strengths, and weaknesses) worked together to keep this student from achieving?

_____

_____

_____

What can you do about it? List strategies that you can employ that would give the students in your class equal access to academic achievement. How can your school community work together to accomplish this?

_____

_____

_____

To reduce achievement gap, affirm diversity, and promote a just distribution of power in our schools, teachers will have to acknowledge existing diversity, accept that it is not going away, and commit to engage in the change or, more precisely, the transition that change requires. Bridges (2003) reminds us, "It isn't the changes that do you in, it's the transition" (p. 3). Elaborating on the significance of this point, Musselwhite (2004) explains, "While change is an event—a death, birth, merger, reorganization, new position, or budget reduction—the human response to change is a process," and this process may "include excitement; heightened emotions such as anxiety, fear, or anger; or even psychological trauma and confusion" (p. 63). Because this transition process does not occur overnight, it requires patience and commitment.

According to people who study change and understand the challenge of transition (e.g., Bridges, 2003; Musselwhite, 2004; Spencer & Adams, 1990), successful transformation requires some kind of change process. Musselwhite and Jones (2003) suggests a process that involves taking four well-defined steps:

1. Acknowledge the change

2. React to the change

3. Investigate the change

4. Implement the change

Each of these steps will be the focus of one of the following four chapters in Section II.

4 Acknowledging the Change/ Transition

Step 1

The first step, acknowledging the change/transition, includes increasing cognitive and emotional awareness. Cognitive awareness may be sparked when teachers hear the principal make an announcement that the school needs to close achievement gaps and affirm diversity. Additionally, both cognitive and emotional awareness may become elevated as actions are taken to implement federal or state legislation aimed at raising academic standards, to refocus the school curriculum on basic knowledge and skills, and to step up accountability measures to assess student learning.

Furthermore, reports in the media about the poor test scores of U.S. students, when compared to students in other parts of the world may raise awareness about the need for change/transition.

4.1 Reflection

Have you noticed a change in the way teachers at your school respond to the achievement gap? If so, what caused this change?

_____

_____

When did it happen?

_____

Compare your observations with a teacher/friend.

_____

_____

4.1 Take Action

Create goals for the change in your school/classroom. Use your answers to the following questions as a starting point.

What do you want to change in your school/classroom?

_____

_____

Explain what you want your school/classroom to look like as it engages in the following:

• Makes changes to reduce the achievement gap
• Affirms and promotes multicultural diversity
• Strives to gives marginalized groups equal access to power

Describe changes that need to be made in the following areas:

• Your school

_____

_____

• Your teaching style

_____

_____

• Your classroom climate

_____

_____

(Continued)

(Continued)

- Your relationships with students with whom you have been unable to connect?

_____

_____

MOBILITY AND CHANGE: A NEW AND DIFFERENT TIME

As previously noted, one reason teachers should affirm diversity is that the demographic profiles of many communities across the United States are changing. Teachers (and teacher educators) do a disservice to students if they construct their teaching expectations around the idea that students will live and work in a single community that will undergo very little change, and that they will live **only** in communities that have similar social and population demographics as the ones in which they grow up. In addition, teachers fail students when they do not acknowledge that we are living in a changing world and help students understand the significance of the changes. In a globalized society that has become more mobile and where jobs are increasingly outsourced, students will likely work in neighborhoods beyond where they attended elementary, middle, and secondary school. Further, teachers cannot predict which of their students will, for example, attend college out of state, live in another country, or volunteer to serve the country by becoming a member of an organization such as the Peace Corps or serve as military personnel in various international locations. Finally, despite the fact that many urban neighborhoods are increasingly segregated—a fact that may seem to argue against teaching for an increasingly diverse society—we do our students who live in segregated communities a great disservice when we fail to prepare them for the rapidly changing world beyond their neighborhood's borders.

To teach students how to work and relate only in racially, ethnically, or linguistically homogeneous sites is to prepare students to fail in a global society. "Us" and "them" thinking is not only detrimental to the well-being of people and institutions; it also ignores that although people may live in the same community and may be of the same socioeconomic and/or racial group, they experience the same community differently and develop different interests. These different ways of experiencing similar experiences and conditions may inspire them to follow very different pathways of thinking and behaving. Some students may seek opportunities to meet with people who represent an aspect of diversity that was not present in their community, while others may purposefully avoid such opportunities.

Not all students or teachers will view diversity as creating life-enriching opportunities; nevertheless, they should be given the opportunity to experience and reflect on diversity because it is a significant part of our current reality.

Through knowing your students, you will come to recognize how willing or unwilling they are to see themselves as threads in the local and global social fabric. However students may see themselves and others, I am suggesting that teachers teach students with the expectation that gradual or immediate change is inevitable. Thomas Friedman (2006) offers an observation that is useful here:

> *Let's face it, my kids have very little chance of working for the same company for twenty-five years, as I have. They have got to be adaptable Swiss Army knives. Gene Sperling, the former economic adviser to President Clinton and author of* The Pro-Growth Progress, *also has a nice way of expressing this. He remarked to me that today's workers need to approach the workplace much like athletes preparing for the Olympics, with one difference. "They have to prepare like someone who is training for the Olympics but doesn't know what sport they are going to enter," said Sperling, "They have to be ready to do anything." (p. 290)*

MULTIPLE TEACHER ROLES AND CHANGE

During the typical teaching day, a teacher wears many hats. Have you recently speculated on the number of different roles that teachers play and how these roles are influenced by the change/transition process? Understanding your roles in a change process is central to your professional welfare during that process, the success of the change taking place, and the smoothness of the transition period. Over the years, the education research literature has argued that the many hats a teacher wears include all of these: director of student learning, friend and counselor to students, member of the teaching profession, school community member, and mediator of culture (Barr, 1950; Grant, 1977; Kinney, 1953; Trow, 1960). For example, as a director of learning—the push toward accountability notwithstanding—teachers influence the curriculum, pedagogy, assessment, who works with whom, and so forth. As a friend and counselor to students, the teacher is a key person who helps students develop their academic "can do" attitude and helps them believe that the school supports their efforts as much as it does any other student's. Similarly, as a member of the school community, the teacher's voice and actions play a significant role in staff meetings and in the teachers' lounge, both of which influence how academic expectations are set for students and the overall spirit of the school. As liaisons between school and community, teachers develop relationships with the students' parents and other community members that influence how the school and community work together to provide for the academic and social needs of the students. In addition, as mediators of culture, teachers instruct students about the values and ideals (e.g., justice, equality) particular to living in a democracy. They also serve as a bridge, helping students to connect to other cultures, languages, lifestyles, and religions that differ from their own.

I am calling attention to the roles that teachers play because some teachers do not fully recognize the many avenues they have to work with students, colleagues, and community members on shrinking the gaps between students who succeed and those who do not.

CHANGING THE MARKERS OF ACHIEVEMENT

Much of the discussion about student achievement in the United States centers on assessments and athletics— the number of points that students receive on their achievement tests or weekly quizzes, or the number of points scored by an athlete or a team. Scores are the major markers of achievement in schools. However, pointing out to students that achievements beyond athletics and academics exist is an important responsibility of teachers. In *The World is Flat*, Friedman (2006) describes how swift and major advances in technology and communication are changing what it takes to make it in the world. Whereas Friedman is very big on students learning technical skills, he is also concerned that students have mental flexibility, self motivation, and psychological mobility (p. 276). He argues that those wishing to work in the new middle-class jobs of the 21st century need to have a "kind of personal touch." Sometimes, this personal dimension is pure passion. At other times, it involves being an entertainer. At still other times, it is a creative touch that no one else thought of adding. But what this personal touch always does is take a routine task and upgrade it to a new middle job (p. 294).

When Friedman was asked about the "right education" young people need to prepare for jobs in the 21st century, he tells of what he learned from interviewing employers and educators. Friedman states, "What they shared with me were not specific courses you should take but rather certain skill sets and attitudes." He lists four examples:

- The ability to learn how to learn—to constantly absorb and teach yourself new ways of doing old things or new ways of doing new things. (p. 302)

- The possession of passion and curiosity, which, "in a flat world, IQ—intelligence quotient—still matters, but CQ and PQ—curiosity quotient and passion quotient—matter even more." (p. 304)
- The ability to manage or interact with other people well. (p. 306)
- The ability to "nurture more of your right brain as well as your left."

"Until recently, the abilities that led to success in school, work and business were characteristic of the left hemisphere. They were the sorts of linear, logical, analytical talents measured by SATS and deployed by CPAs. Today, these capabilities are still necessary. But they're no longer sufficient. In a world upended by outsourcing, deluged with data, and choked with choices, the abilities that matter most are now closer in spirit to the specialties of the right hemisphere—artistry, empathy, seeing the big picture and pursuing the transcendent." (p. 307)

4.2 Reflection

I find Friedman's (2006) statement about the importance of a curiosity quotient and passion quotient (p. 304) illuminating. It demands a response to the following questions:

Where and how do students develop curiosity and passion?

_____

_____

_____

How can we shift the emphasis in teaching so the focus on helping students is twofold, scoring well on high-stakes tests and helping students develop curiosity and passion?

_____

_____

_____

5 Reacting to Change/Transition

Step 2

"Change" doesn't need managing as much as do the people involved with the change.

—Chris Musselwhite (2004, p. 61)

Once teachers are cognitively and emotionally aware of the change that their society is undergoing, they begin reacting to that change. A successful transition involves letting go of the way things used to be and taking hold of the way they subsequently become. In between the letting go and the taking hold again, there is a chaotic but potentially creative "neutral zone" when things are not the old way but are not really a new way either. Thus, transition is a three-phrase process: ending, neutral zone, and beginning again (Bridges, 2003). In this section, I address five reactions to change/transition in schools and how they relate to the three-phase process described by Bridges: strong feeling and mixed emotion, search to connect with student knowledge and experiences, nervous reaction to racism and other "isms," reactions influenced by the context and settings, and new teachers need help.

5.1 Take Action

Create a list of the individual strengths your students bring to the classroom. Focus on both academic and nonacademic strengths. Is there a student whose constant chatter is really a sign of a lively, engaged mind? Is there a student who drums on the table during independent work time but, when allowed to use her hands to fix or create something, is engaged and productive?

How can you encourage students to develop and make the most of their strengths? How can you help all of the students in your class to value and use their strengths when working together so that the achievement of all students is heightened?

Make a plan to highlight an individual student's strengths each day this week. Plan an activity that gives that specific student a leadership role, allowing the student to showcase and/or teach other students about his or her strength.

If you are struggling with how to change your instruction in order to make space for all of your students' many and diverse talents, complex instruction is one way to start. Complex instruction is one method of cooperative learning that is often highly successful in heterogeneous, diverse classrooms. It is based on six central tenets:

1. Classroom tasks should always require multiple ability orientations; tasks assigned require a group to draw on multiple intelligences and abilities in order to accomplish difficult thinking tasks. To be successful, a group will have to draw on the strengths and skills of each member.

2. These tasks must be group worthy, or complex and difficult enough to warrant a group's collaboration. A simple group task will not be successful. Rather, a task must be centered on authentic, real-world questions; there should be multiple ways of approaching and solving the problem or task; and it should be open-ended.

3. Teachers must actively work to assign competence to all students or to break down status hierarchies by explicitly showing each group the skills and talents that each member brings.

4. For groups to work successfully, the teacher must actively work to create a community with positive norms. Complex instruction requires that a classroom know how to work positively together and that the class members hold one another responsible for abiding by these norms.

5. As with cooperative learning in general, complex instruction requires that a group's roles be intertwined. Tasks should require positive interdependence (everyone depends on everyone else to complete the task), individual accountability (there is a system for grading/assessing each individual's understanding and contribution), equal participation (each person's role is of equal importance),

(Continued)

(Continued)

> and simultaneous interaction (everyone participates at the same time).
>
> 6. Finally, there must be authentic, higher-order assessments. A test, for example, is an inadequate assessment of complex instruction. Rather, everything the group does should be building toward the assessment, which likely requires the students to construct or create something.
>
> For more on complex instruction, see Elizabeth Cohen and Rachel Lotan's *Working for Equity in Heterogeneous Classrooms: Sociological Theory in Action* (1997); the *Program for Complex Instruction at Stanford University* (see http://cgi.stanford.edu/group/pci/cgi-bin/site.cgi?page=index.html); or Watanabe, Nunes, Mebane, Scalise, and Claesgens (2007) in *Chemistry for All, Instead of Chemistry Just for the Elite*: *Lessons Learned from Detracked Chemistry Classrooms.*"

STRONG FEELING AND MIXED EMOTIONS

Transition is a process that "includes excitement; heightened emotions such as anxiety, fear, or anger; or even psychological trauma and confusion" (Musselwhite, 2004, p. 63). During the reacting stage, your emotions and those of your colleagues may become intense. Strong feelings (e.g., anger, joy) or mixed emotions (e.g., indifference) may develop. The emotional reactions may be accompanied by behaviors such as withdrawal, collaboration, or inaction.

When teachers resist transition, they resist one or more of the three phrases of its makeup: letting go of the old, being in between, or making a risky new beginning. Teachers resist transition not because they cannot accept change, but because they cannot accept giving up that piece of themselves that the changed situation requires (Bridges, 2003).

During the reaction stage, I have heard statements such as these:

- I have been teaching here for the past 25 years. Why do we have to change the way we have been teaching? These parents should see that their children come to school ready to learn. All these students and their families should learn English.
- Finally, we are going to educate ALL of the students in this school!
- It is hard to have high expectations for the at-risk students in my class. I know most of them are not going to college. So why upset them? I am satisfied when they are being quiet instead of being discipline problems.

In the reacting phase, teachers should not be surprised or disappointed if they cannot immediately agree on how to deal with achievement gaps and the affirmation of diversity. Some staff members will be open to some ideas about diversity but not others. You may encounter teacher/friends who support equal rights and argue that children of color must have a first-class education but who remain silent on gay and lesbian issues in education. As you and other staff members bring forth new ideas about the affirmation of diversity and achievement gaps in your schools, these ideas will increase the complexity of the transition process.

Change is not neat, clean, or immediate. The call for change may cause an initial reaction by some staff members that there is not enough time, that people don't have the energy, or that the quality and quantity of individual and institutional resources are insufficient. The challenge is to move beyond the reacting phase by creating a plan to implement change.

SEARCHING TO CONNECT WITH STUDENT KNOWLEDGE AND EXPERIENCES

Teachers come to the change/transition process with resources (knowledge, skills, and attitudes) that can help eliminate achievement gaps and affirm diversity or, conversely, maintain achievement gaps and ignore diversity. Helping teachers constructively use their resources during the reacting phase includes helping them connect with the knowledge students have as well as understanding how diverse students learn through their own particular cultured lenses.

To illustrate how teachers may connect with the knowledge base students already bring to the classroom, let's return to Delpit's (1996) illustration in Chapter 2 (pp. 26–27) and also consider the teacher's role as a mediator of culture. Delpit's example is a reminder that teachers benefit from knowing about significant traditions, folklore, and ways of behaving within students' cultural group(s). These indigenous forms of knowing and acting can inform school curricula and instruction in ways that improve students' academic achievement, especially when teachers model an understanding of and respect for them.

On the other hand, teachers who see themselves as experts rather than learners when tackling achievement gaps will miss out on opportunities to connect with students' knowledge and experience. It is therefore wiser for teachers to see themselves as facilitators in the change/transition process who create "a classroom climate that allows for a constructive exchange of ideas and experiences" (Álvarez & Miville, 2003, p. 532).

NERVOUS REACTIONS TO RACISM AND OTHER "ISM"S

When racism comes up in one of its many manifestations—as in a word or a racist act—a nervous reaction often occurs. Such reactions require

teachers to demonstrate patience, speak the truth, permit different view-
points to be heard, and maintain a climate of respect for all. Nervous reactions to racism relate to other forms of anxiety that emerge when teachers
do any of the following:

- Confront their own identity conflicts
- Confront or are confronted with their own biases
- Respond to biased comments
- Grapple with their own imperfect cultural competency
- Want the approval of students and peers
- Facilitate intense emotional conflict (Weinstein & Obear, 1992)

Effectively working through such anxiety requires that teachers remain
"open to acknowledging both to themselves and to their students, their
own socialization process and the continuous unlearning and relearning
that accompanies this awareness" (Álvarez & Miville, 2003, p. 542). At one
time, I had difficulty eating lunch with students who had muscular dys-
trophy because, in some cases, the saliva would run down their cheeks and
some students chewed their food with their mouths open. With some
"talking to myself" and talking with a teacher/friend who compassion-
ately told me that she, too, had had to learn to work through similar experiences, I got a grip on my reaction. This learning experience helped me to
be more empathetic and compassionate when working with others who
are struggling with race or sexuality.

In addition, teachers and students may glean insight from anxiety-
inducing events by comparing and contrasting them to events in their own
experience. More specifically, "It may be helpful for instructors to reflect on
those areas in their own lives that they still find challenging and how they
may be manifested in their teaching" (Álvarez & Miville, 2003, p. 542). A
personal example here may be helpful. Often as a graduate student and now
as a professor, I am in academic and social settings where I am the only
person of color or one of the very few people of color. These experiences are,
on some occasions, very challenging because of, for example, the anxiety
or pressure to represent my race well. On occasion, I use the background
stories that give context to these personal challenges in my teaching to help
undergraduate and graduate students to better understand and appreciate
the continuous struggles they will face as they act to affirm diversity.

REACTIONS ARE INFLUENCED
BY CONTEXT AND SETTINGS

Killen, McGlothlin, and Henning (2007) argue, "Beliefs about groups
change across contexts ... and ... beliefs about members of *out groups*

vary depending on the situation" (p. 3). For example, racial biases in one setting, such as a fearful reaction to a group of large Black boys that you see while jogging, differ from racial attitudes in another setting, such as an annoyed reaction to a group of large Black boys in the school hallway whom you tell to get to class as the bell rings. Dealing with diversity concepts (e.g., racism) that are multifaceted and emerge in different ways depending on the circumstance requires honesty with yourself and a willingness to grow.

The jogging example comes from Joyce, a teacher who shared the story with me. Joyce realized that she shows no fear of any student while in school but was perplexed by her out-of-school behavior and wanted to address it. I suggested that she consult with the school district social worker to see if other teachers have reported experiencing similar feelings and were seeking help. If so, staff development could be arranged to help teachers. My point here is that if circumstances arise that may have deeper manifestations, professional help should be sought.

NEW TEACHERS NEED HELP

Before leaving this discussion on reactions, a reminder for the experienced teachers at the school may be in order. Beginning teachers who join the faculty may come with only a minimal understanding of how to affirm diversity and will need help. According to the U.S. Department of Education, 75 percent of the teaching force is female and 84 percent are White (Snyder, Tan, & Hoffman, 2004). According to the American Association of College Teacher Education (AACTE; 2003), new teachers often feel unprepared to deliver effective instruction to the multicultural population they teach, and many are not deeply committed to more than a superficial concept of diversity that centers on food, fairs, and festivals. Helping new teachers to develop a more informed and positive perspective about affirming diversity may therefore be a challenge. Consider the following statement from Lisa Delpit (1996):

> We say that we believe that all children can learn, but few of us really believe it. Teacher education usually focuses on research that links failure and socioeconomic status, failure and cultural difference, and failure and single-parent households. It is hard to believe that these children can possibly be successful after their teachers have been so thoroughly exposed to so much negative indoctrination. When teachers receive that kind of education, there is a tendency to assume deficits in students rather than to locate and teach to strengths. To counter this tendency, educators must have knowledge of children's lives outside of school so as to recognize their strengths. (p. 172)

Action Plan 5: Reacting to the Change: Confronting Our Biases and Conditioning

I. This week, I will ask you to take a (perhaps uncomfortable) look at your conditioned biases. Think back to the experiences from Week 4, when you went "apartment hunting" with your friend. Expand your knowledge by paying specific attention to ways in which the power structures in your school district, the influence of the media, and so forth manifest themselves. If you are struggling with seeing these subtleties, again, ask a friend from a culture different than your own to process through this with you. You may also wish to watch a movie such as *Crash* or *Do the Right Thing* and review the responses to it.

II. Next, examine your own experiences. This may be uncomfortable. None of us likes to admit these things. However, identifying biases is important to moving on from them. If you are a White person, you may feel helpless, as though you cannot do anything to combat these societal influences. However, after identifying the answers to the following questions, consider that, as a society, we can only move forward if we can all work together, regardless of differences, to effect change. And you, as a teacher, have a large amount of agency and influence in this process.

Discuss a time when you received the "benefit of the doubt" based on your race, gender, class or other social marker:

_____

_____

_____

Discuss a time when you may have "gotten ahead" at the expense of another human being:

_____

_____

_____

III. Consider that perhaps our society's values may have encouraged you to develop an identity based on the feeling of being superior to others. (Think about how hard it is to admit when another teacher does something "better" than you.) Discuss a time when you perhaps fulfilled your own need to feel "good enough" by causing someone else to feel "less than":

_____

_____

_____

IV. This week, practice what you have been "preaching" in your classroom, collegiality and working together. Ask a colleague whom you admire to explain techniques with a certain subject matter or teaching strategy. Ask questions and state your admiration for this person. How did this experience affect you?

_____

_____

_____

V. Next, practice partnering with others in the community. Visit a church, synagogue, mosque, temple, day care center, or even a parent in the community where you teach. Ask the people you meet there about their hopes for the children they serve. Ask their opinion on how you, as the children's teacher, can help them strive to reach these goals. How has this changed you? These conversations changed me in the following ways:

_____

_____

_____

6 Investigating the Change/Transition and Self

Step 3

To exist is to change, to change is to mature, to mature is to go on creating oneself endlessly.

—Henri Bergson (n.d.)

Movement into investigating the change/transition phase marks the movement from a past to a present orientation. In our present orientation, we see that demographic diversity is increasing, globalization is enduring, technology is making the world flat (interdependence), achievement gaps are persisting, and the affirmation of cultural diversity is still a dream (with a bit more hope included). So the investigating stage is the time to analyze and come up with an action plan to address changes and transition as they are experienced. This action plan should manifest itself in two forms: self-investigating and program investigating.

In the self-investigating area, it is important for teachers to evaluate how well they are doing in their efforts to close achievement gaps and affirm diversity. Self-investigating can draw on reflective questions that examine teachers' progress in understanding how gaps like poverty and limited access to health care act together to influence students' school performance. Reflective questions should look at the extent that teachers use culturally responsive teaching strategies, that they use multicultural/social justice curricula, and that they recognize power relations. At a deeper level, reflective questions may include, "Does my teaching explicitly and implicitly attempt to justify the exercise of power by those who possess it while striving to reconcile the fact that others do not have the same opportunities to exercise power?" Illustrations of such teaching may occur, for example, when teachers teach the Westward Movement and the role of women in science. A teacher may teach the Westward Movement from a historical European perspective of presenting it as a hardship—surviving in the "wilderness" and fending off the "wild Indians," while the perspective of the Native Americans whose land and lives were stolen is given little, if any, attention, and the diminished exercise of power Native Americans had (and have) is justified. Likewise, studying the role of women in science by teaching a special unit reduces women's contributions to science to "novelty" and downplays women's integral role in the advancement of many scientific fields.

Ponterotto, Blanch, Greig and Rivera (1998) have published a Teacher Multicultural Attitude Survey (TMAS) that includes three different sets of statements concerning teachers' personal dispositions, knowledge, and skills. Because answering questions in the three surveys and discussing them with a small group of teacher/friends may help teachers to gain valuable personal insights about their views toward multiculturalism and the teaching of it, one of the surveys is included in each of the next three chapters of this book.

The first survey is about teachers' multicultural attitudes. Record a response of agree or disagree to complete the survey and then share your responses with a teacher/friend. Discuss why you agree or disagree with the statements below.

TEACHER MULTICULTURAL ATTITUDE SURVEY (TMAS)

1. I find teaching a culturally diverse student group rewarding.

   Agree   Disagree

2. Teaching methods need to be adapted to meet the needs of a culturally diverse student group.

   Agree   Disagree

3. Sometimes I think there is too much emphasis placed on multicultural awareness and training for teachers.

   Agree   Disagree

4. Teachers have the responsibility to be aware of their students' cultural backgrounds.

   Agree   Disagree

5. I frequently invite extended family members (e.g., cousins, grand-parents, godparents) to attend parent. teacher conferences.

   Agree   Disagree

6. It is not the teacher's responsibility to encourage pride in one's culture.

   Agree   Disagree

7. As classrooms become more culturally diverse, the teacher's job becomes increasingly challenging.

   Agree   Disagree

8. I believe the teacher's role needs to be redefined to address the needs of students from culturally diverse backgrounds.

   Agree   Disagree

9. When dealing with bilingual students, some teachers may misinterpret different communication styles as behavioral problems.

   Agree   Disagree

10. As classrooms become more culturally diverse, the teacher's job becomes increasingly rewarding.

    Agree   Disagree

11. I can learn a great deal from students with culturally different backgrounds.

    Agree   Disagree

12. Multicultural training for teachers is not necessary.

    Agree   Disagree

13. In order to be an effective teacher, one needs to be aware of cultural differences present in the classroom.

    Agree   Disagree

14. Multicultural-awareness training can help me work more effectively with a diverse student population.

    Agree   Disagree

15. Students should learn to communicate in English only.

    Agree   Disagree

16. Today's curriculum gives undue importance to multiculturalism and diversity.

    Agree   Disagree

17. I am aware of the diversity of cultural backgrounds in my classroom.

    Agree   Disagree

18. Regardless of the racial and ethnic makeup of my class, it is important for all students to be aware of multicultural diversity.

   Agree   Disagree

19. Being multiculturally aware is not relevant for the subject I teach.

   Agree   Disagree

20. Teaching students about cultural diversity will only create conflict in the classroom.

   Agree   Disagree

SOURCE: For detailed information on these Ponterotto © Instruments, see:

Ponterotto, J. G., Utsey, S. O., & Pederson, P. B. (2006). *Preventing prejudice: A guide for counselors, educators, and parents* (2nd ed.). Thousand Oaks, CA: Sage.

Ponterotto, J. G., Mendelsohn, J., & Belizaire, L. (2003). Assessing teacher multicultural competence: Self-report instruments, observer-report evaluations, and a portfolio assessment. In D. P. Pope-Davis, H. L. K. Coleman, R. Toporek, & W. Liu (Eds.), *Handbook of multicultural competencies in counseling and psychology* (pp. 191–210). Thousand Oaks, Sage.

If you find yourself disagreeing with statements 1, 2, 3, 4, 8, 9, 10, 11, 13, 14, 17 or 18, you may still be expecting your diverse student body to conform to the values, communication styles, and languages of the "culture of power" (Delpit, 1996) in U.S. society. Holding on to these attitudes may prevent your students, not only from developing pride in their own cultures but also from gaining access to the mainstream discourse that they will need as they make their way in the world.

While working on this book, a teacher, Beth, asked me, "What can I do to motivate a colleague who is not interested in engaging in personal change?" My response to Beth's question—a question I have heard numerous times—draws on the much-quoted work about planning change by Chin and Benne (1976). They identified three strategies for effecting change with people: rational/empirical, power/coercive and normative/reeducative. Although space does not permit detailed discussion of these three strategies, I will address them briefly.

Rational/empirical strategies are based on the assumption that people are rational and will follow their rational self-interest once it is revealed to them. In Beth's case, this strategy means identifying for her teacher/friend a connection between affirming diversity and something in which she is invested, like getting the accountability monitors off of her back. In other words, once Beth's teacher/friend recognizes how affirming diversity can help to improve her students' test scores, she will be more likely to buy into the process of self-investigating. Power/coercive strategies involve having "authority of law or administrative policy behind the change to be effected" (Chin & Benne, 1976, p. 24). For Beth, this could mean asking the principal to speak out at a faculty meeting about the importance (and requirement) of all teachers' active participation in the change/transition process and/or to set up concrete benchmarks and a plan of evaluation.

Normative/reeducative strategies are founded on the assumption that change "will occur only as the persons involved are brought to change their normative orientations of old patterns and develop commitments to new ones" (Chin & Benne, 1976, p. 23). This strategy further assumes "changes in attitudes, values, skills and significant relationships, not just changes in knowledge, information, or intellectual rationales for action and practice" (p. 23). It is the normative/reeducative strategies that I would recommend Beth use to help her teacher/friend become active in closing achievement gaps and affirming diversity. This recommendation is based on the belief that individual and group norms influence individual and group behaviors and attitudes. Consequently, teachers in Beth's situation will need to use strategies that help colleagues adopt and affirm new norms that demonstrate respect for all people. This may include sharing lesson plans, books, articles, film, and telling stories that successfully address the change underway.

Teachers can correctly be described as the lynchpin to success in closing achievement gaps and affirming diversity regardless of the ethnic/racial makeup of their classrooms. I base this statement on a question from Mimi, a teacher in a suburban school where the student population is mostly White. Mimi asked me, "If our school is not having a problem with the achievement gap and we are 98 percent White and Protestant, do we need to be concerned about affirming diversity?" Mimi's question is a good one. It emerges from the assumption that diversity and multicultural education are just for people of color. My response to Mimi was, "Teachers should remember that if their students are predominately White and middle class, they are responsible for teaching in a way that does not give license to White privilege and abuse of unequal power structures. White, middle-class students should develop an identity that is not based on feeling superior to people of color and does not assume that other cultures are inferior because they are different. Also White, middle-class students do not know where they will live or work as adults; therefore, it is wise for them to prepare for sending most of their time is a diverse society. In addition, the United States has always prized the diverse makeup of its citizens. Therefore, it is essential that students in any and all schools learn to affirm diversity."

KNOWLEDGE OF SELF: SELF-UNDERSTANDING AND SELF-ACCEPTANCE

In the 1950s, Arthur Jersild conducted research on the relation between self-understanding and education. He asked, "How does helping students in a distinctly intimate and personal way influence the teacher's own life?" He concluded, "The teacher's understanding and acceptance of himself (*sic*) is the most important requirement in any effort he makes to help students to know themselves and to gain healthy attitudes of self-acceptance" (Jersild, 1955, p. 12). Researchers today continue to support Jersild's thesis by suggesting that teachers' ability to critically analyze themselves and their life experiences is crucial to understanding their students. Palmer (1998), for example, argues that self-knowledge is not optional but, rather, absolutely essential for good teaching. Speaking about his own teaching, he argues, "Knowing myself is as crucial to good teaching as knowing my students and my subject. In fact, knowing my students and my subject depends heavily on self-knowledge" (p. 2).

Because classrooms are places of struggle over what is good for students where competing debates are in play (e.g., state-mandated, high-stakes tests versus parental support of multiple assessment types), teachers should have a clear understanding about their beliefs and be able to support their beliefs with research and good practice evidence. I am aware that teachers sometimes have to adhere to the "party line"; nevertheless, discussions with parents, for example, can be more helpful to the parents and teacher if, while continuing to support the party line, the teacher can offer parents an alternative based upon their professional beliefs that is supported by research and good practice data. An example here may be useful. Consider the story of Ernest, a fifth-grade student. Ernest's parents had been invited to have him undergo an assessment to see if a special education placement would be good for him. After the parents gave permission and the assessment was completed, it was time to meet with Ernest's parents. Marge, Ernest's teacher, the Building Consultation Team (principal, nurse, school psychologist, school social worker, special education teacher, speech and language teacher and home/school coordinator), and Ernest's parents met to discuss the results of the assessment. The Building Consultation Team recommended placing Ernest in special education. The team contended that Ernest met the profile of a student who needs the care a special education class can provide. The aid in Marge's classroom supported the recommendation and two other teachers, math and music, believed that he was a candidate for special education and supported the idea. Marge, however, said she was unsure about the idea. Ernest's parents were in a quandary; they did not believe, based on Ernest's behavior and attitude toward school-type learning at home, that he should be placed in special education. However, they wanted to do the right thing by him and were somewhat overwhelmed and in awe of the Building Consultation Team. Marge said, "I believe that because the suggestions to place Ernest in special education were coming from all of the professionals, it blew the parents away." They, however, told the team, "We need to think this over." Marge went on to say, "As I walked Ernest's parents to the door, I told them that if they wanted to, they could seek a second opinion from a private psychologist. They thanked me and left. A month later, Ernest's mother called me and reported that, although they had to pay for a private psychologist, they learned that Ernest was a "normal" child. In fact, Ernest's mother said, "The psychologist who tested him first words to us, were, 'Why is he here?'" Marge added that when the team received the report from the psychologist, some were more concerned about what led Ernest's parents to consult a private psychologist than the excellent test results Ernest received. A footnote to this story may be satisfying because I am often asked, "Is there a race or diversity component to this story?" Maybe. Ernest is a Black male, and many Black males are disproportionately placed in special education (Blanchett, 2006). However, we don't know if Ernest's race encouraged the aid and the math and music teacher to recommend that he should meet with the Building Consultation Team. Also, Ernest's parents are middle class; having the financial capability probably allowed Ernest's parents not to have to wait and for him to be examined by a private psychologist.

On some occasions, cultures and lifestyles (yours and your students' families) may clash in the classroom. Haberman (1995) posits, "To some degree, all of us are socialized to regard our culture group(s) as superior to others. Our group may be based upon race, religion, language, gender, class, or all of the above" (p. 7). Haberman's statement suggests that teachers who teach to close achievement gaps should consider how their beliefs about their own cultural group(s) and beliefs about those of others may affect the way they approach the teaching/learning process. Understanding oneself also includes understanding how one's self-identified and ascribed characteristics (e.g., ethnicity, class, gender, disability) influence teaching. As Delpit (1996) argues, "One of the most difficult tasks as a human being is communicating meaning across our individual differences, a task confounded immeasurably as we attempt to communicate across social lines, ethnic lines, cultural lines, or lines of unequal power" (p. 10).

Weiner's (1993) research on social class deepens our understanding of the effects of social characteristics on teaching. She believes that teachers from working-class homes are more susceptible to institutional pressures to conform than are candidates from high-status homes. More specifically, Weiner, as well as Zumwalt and Craig (2008), contend that because many young, White, working-class women are the first members of their family to attend college, they are interested in teaching as a permanent, professional home. As first-generation professionals, teachers from working-class homes are more apt to comply with traditional education practices than challenge practices that reproduce unequal outcomes. In short, Weiner found that these teachers tended to passively accept the status quo.

6.1 Reflection

What do you think of the statements by Haberman, Delpit, and Weiner?

_____

_____

What parts of the statement do you agree with?

_____

_____

In what ways do you agree?

_____

_____

What parts don't you agree with?

_____

_____

In what ways do you disagree?

_____

_____

Share your thoughts with a teacher/friend. (This time, have them treat you to a cup of coffee, tea, or hot chocolate.)

Self-acceptance and a strong identity help us to feel comfortable "in our own skin" and better able to deal with the world around us. Tatum (1997) argues that one reason Black students sometimes sit away from other kids in the cafeteria is not because they are hostile or wish to be separatists but because Black adolescents are displaying signs of growing self-acceptance. Similarly, a teacher who has a strong sense of identity will be more likely to examine the flow of power between teacher and students, including effects of power on students' sense of their own self-worth and that of others, without fearing the criticism of other teachers. In addition, teachers with a strong sense of identity are better able to participate in the give-and-take in the change/transition process. As debates rage over curriculum, instruction, standards, and testing, teachers who do not feel confident taking a stand on educational issues may find it difficult to participate in conversations about closing achievement gaps and affirming diversity. Teachers with a strong sense of self, on the other hand, will more easily engage in conversation with other faculty members, offer suggestions, respond to disagreements, and thereby contribute to the improvement of their schools.

MULTICULTURAL PERSONALITY FOR AFFIRMING DIVERSITY

Much of the counseling, psychology, and education literature are in fairly close agreement that people who work in service-providing professions need to assess their attitudes toward, knowledge of, and skills for working with the people whom they serve. This self-evaluation is especially important in light of recent shifts in the manifestations of bigotry, particularly the replacement of crude, overtly discriminatory practices with a more subtle and amorphous "new racism" in organizations and institutions (Howitt & Owusu-Bempah, 1990). Helping professionals would be well served to develop a multicultural personality, which Ponterotto, Mendelsohn, and Belizaire (2003) define as

> *being characterized by an individual who embraces diversity in her or his personal life; makes active attempts to learn about other cultures and interact with culturally different people (e.g., friends, colleagues); understands the biases inherent in his or her own worldview and actively learns about alternate worldviews; and is a social activist, empowered to speak out against all forms of social injustice (e.g., racism, homophobia, sexism, ageism, domestic violence, religious stereotyping). (p. 200)*

6.2 Reflection

To what extent is the Ponterotto et al. (2003) definition of a multicultural personality consistent with your own?

not consistent   somewhat consistent   consistent   very consistent

Discuss the Ponterotto et al. (2003) definition with two or three teacher/friends (including a new teacher).

You may wish to start by sharing some of your reactions to the definition. For example, the definition covers four areas of diversity: (1) diversity in your personal life, (2) interactions with culturally different people, (3) biases in your own worldview, and (4) your social action. Starting with comments about the nature and quality of diversity in your personal life will get the ball rolling. This can be followed up with the question, "What kinds of interactions have you had over the past six months with a person who is culturally different from you?"

To what extent do the following statements in the Teacher Personal Dispositions Toward Diversity Survey (Ponterotto et al., 1998) apply to you?

_____

_____

TEACHER PERSONAL DISPOSITIONS TOWARD DIVERSITY SURVEY

1. I understand that becoming a multicultural teacher is a continuous process that all teachers must address. I personally have progressed in my development by moving from being less culturally aware to becoming more aware and sensitive to my own cultural heritage and to valuing and respecting differences. I am aware how my own cultural background and experiences, attitudes, values, and biases influence my views of education and social processes.

   Greatly apply   Somewhat apply   Do not apply

2. I am comfortable with differences that exist between students and me in race, ethnicity, culture, gender, sexual orientation, beliefs, and so on. Part of this process includes recognizing my preconceived notions, stereotypes, and negative emotional reactions toward historically oppressed groups (as well as other groups) and understanding how these reactions may prove detrimental to my students in their education and social development. I am willing to contrast many beliefs and attitudes with those of my culturally different students in a nonjudgmental fashion.

   Greatly apply   Somewhat apply   Do not apply

3. I possess knowledge and understanding about how oppression, racism, discrimination, and stereotyping affect me personally and in my work. In addition to recognizing how I am discriminated against based on my group memberships, I acknowledge my own discriminatory attitudes, beliefs, and feelings about race, sexual orientation, class, gender, and so on. I understand how I may have experienced privilege in my own life and how I may have directly or indirectly benefited from individual, institutional, and cultural racism/sexism.

   Greatly apply   Somewhat apply   Do not apply

4. As a teacher, I am aware that I have the potential for tremendous social influence on my students, as well as their families. As an employee of the board of education, I recognize the education system and the school as being extremely powerful socializing agents. I also understand how this socializing process may act to oppress minorities.

   Greatly apply   Somewhat apply   Do not apply

5. I view diversity in my classroom as an asset to my students' education, as well as my own. I understand diversity benefits the learning of all the students in my classroom. I am aware of the need, and have the ability to incorporate the multitude of human experiences in my lesson plans and course materials.

   Greatly apply   Somewhat apply   Do not apply

6. I am committed to becoming more socially active to fight oppression in my classroom, my school, my community, and my personal life.

   Greatly apply   Somewhat apply   Do not apply

SOURCE: For detailed information on these Ponterotto © Instruments, see:

Ponterotto, J. G., Utsey, S. O., & Pederson, P. B. (2006). *Preventing prejudice: A guide for counselors, educators, and parents* (2nd ed.). Thousand Oaks, CA: Sage.

Ponterotto, J. G., Baluch, S., Greig, T., & Rivera, L. (1998). Development and initial validation of the Teacher Multicultural Attitude Survey (TMAS). *Educational and Psychological Measurement, 58,* 1002–1016.

6.3 Reflection

Give examples of the things you already do that are listed in the Teacher Personal Dispositions Toward Diversity Survey.

_____

_____

If you are lacking in certain areas, write out how you can develop your dispositions in those areas.

_____

_____

Discuss the Ponterotto et al. (2003) definition with two or three teacher/friends (including a new teacher).

Discuss with your teacher/friends how you achieved and developed your personal dispositions toward diversity.

_____

_____

KNOWLEDGE ABOUT THE SCHOOL COMMUNITY SURVEY

How well do you know the community where you teach? This is a key question because, as a teacher, you serve both the students and the community. A few years ago, the phrase "it takes a village to raise a child" was a popular statement echoed throughout the United States. Moreover, Ladson-Billings (1994) describes teachers with a positive self-identity as those who see themselves as a part of the community and who see teaching as giving back to the community. These ideas have currency and support the view that teachers and students will benefit when teachers become active in the community where they teach.

How would you answer the following questions about teachers' attitudes and dispositions?

ATTITUDES AND DISPOSITIONS OF TEACHERS WHO WORK TO CLOSE THE ACHIEVEMENT GAP SURVEY

1. Do you believe that all children are capable of high-quality learning and achievement?

   Yes   No

2. Do you believe in holding high expectations for all students regardless of their life circumstances?

   Yes   No

3. Do you trust all of your students?

    No   A few   Mostly all   All

4. Do you believe that all parents want what is best for their children, even if they may not be sure of how to help them achieve success?

    No   A few   Mostly all   All

5. Do you believe that as a teacher you have the power to make a significant difference in the lives of your students?

    No   Somewhat   Mostly yes   Very much so

6. Are you willing to teach students regardless of their ethnicity, gender, sexual orientation, cultural practices, and socioeconomic status?

    Reluctant   Somewhat reluctant   Yes

7. Do you think of teaching as a job or a career?

    Job   Career

8. When you look out at your class of students, where do you see them in fifteen years?

_____

_____

6.4 Reflection

Are you satisfied with your comments on the Attitudes and Dispositions of Teachers Who Work to Close the Achievement Gap Survey? Discuss your comments with a teacher/friend.

6.5 Reflection

Discuss Haberman's (1995) statements with a teacher/friend, especially a teacher who has transferred from another school or district or is a beginning teacher. Beginning teachers, especially, may like to have someone with whom to discuss these ideas. Consider becoming their mentor.

6.1 Take Action

To expand your knowledge of differing communication styles among cultures, strengthen a friendship you have with someone from a culture different than your own. Ask the person to observe you teaching and to watch for moments of miscommunication and good communication between you and the students. Upon receiving feedback, use this information to inform your teaching. As a bonus, ask the person to accompany you to a social gathering that people who are different from yourself are attending and where you may observe various communication styles in action. This could be a barbeque, a live music event, or some other activity. Don't view attending the event as research; strive to become a friend and to enjoy yourself and increase your understanding of diversity.

Haberman (1995) lists twelve characteristics that both beginning and veteran teachers agree are meaningful for all teachers. Haberman states "star" teachers are characterized by the following:

1. Tend to be nonjudgmental. As they interact with children and adults in schools, their first thought is not to decide the goodness of things but to understand events and communications.

2. Are not moralistic. They don't believe that teaching is preaching.

3. Are not easily shocked by horrific events. They tend to ask, "What can I do about this?" and if they think they can help, they do; otherwise, they get on with their work and their lives.

4. Not only listen, they hear. They not only hear, but they seek to understand. They regard listening to children, parents, or anyone involved in the school community as a potential source of information.

5. Recognize that they have feelings of hate, prejudice, and bias and strive to overcome them.

6. Do not see themselves as saviors who have come to save their schools. They hold a servant-leader attitude.

7. Do not see themselves as being alone. They network.

8. See themselves as "winning," even though they know their total influence on their students is much less than that of total society, neighborhood, and gangs.

9. Enjoy their interactions with children and youth so much that they are willing to put up with the irrational demands of the school system.

10. Think their primary impact on students is that they have made them more humane and less frustrated, or raised their self-esteem.

11. Derive all types of satisfactions and meet all kinds of needs by teaching children and youth. The one exception is power; they meet no power needs whatsoever by functioning as teachers. (p. 93)

Action Plan 6: Self-Investigation

I. This week you are to search for miscommunications that may take place in your classroom. Before you invite a colleague to observe and discuss the communication styles in your classroom, you may want to experience what it feels like to be on the side of trying to understand someone whose communication style differs from your own. Try asking someone who speaks a language you do not understand to tell you how to complete a step-by-step activity in the language you do not know, such as finding directions to the local grocery store. List the results of this experience:

_____

_____

_____

_____

Next, list the results of your work on miscommunication with your colleague in your classroom:

_____

_____

_____

_____

How will these new experiences and knowledge inform your teaching in the future?

_____

_____

_____

_____

7 Investigating the Change/Transition

Program Investigation

Program investigating has as its purpose evaluating how well a school is addressing achievement gaps and affirming diversity. Much like self-investigating, program investigating includes "adjudication"—that is, having members of the program take a close look at programmatic structures and policies and determining the extent of its progress toward equity. The policies that influence the affirmation of diversity may include resource distribution practices (e.g., whether or not faculty of color, bilingual teachers, and/or community-based paraprofessionals are hired). More specifically, schools' promotion of racial, ethnic, and gender diversity when offering employment and other opportunities is a key to shaping the social climate and members' perceptions of intergroup relations (Kossek & Zonia 1993). In addition, Kossek and Zonia (1993) argue that social group affiliations are often more powerful than contextual characteristics when discussing differences in diversity attitudes. In other words, teachers' race or lifestyles may affect their knowledge and attitudes about school policy and practice more so than the needs and the conditions the students at the school are facing.

Program investigation begins with an inquiry—an activity that teachers may conduct using the questions below and which teachers may want to add to—into which actions are being taken to move the change/transition process forward. For example, program investigation raises questions like these:

1. As a school, how far have we come with our knowledge, skills, and attitudes about achievement gaps and diversity?

2. To which instructional and curriculum contexts (e.g., student centered versus teacher centered; school centered versus parent centered) have we devoted most of our time and attention?

3. Have all of the staff members taken the multicultural awareness, knowledge, and skills survey?

4. Have we set goals, identified benchmarks, and mapped out a timetable for closing achievement gaps and affirming diversity?

5. Do we have a committee or other organizational structure in place to assist the change process?

6. How do we determine (not assume) the particular achievement gaps that the students have?

7. How do we determine (not assume) both the in-school and out-of-school challenges that students are facing?

8. Do we have a structure and criteria in place to evaluate the school's progress?

Program investigating also means being more perceptive (but not snoopy!) about your colleagues' attitudes and behaviors. For example, some social psychologists argue that individuals may mask racial and other biases in order to tell people what they think they want to hear (Killen et al., 2007). Accordingly, these social psychologists seek to understand the contradictory behaviors and beliefs that allow individuals to "hold implicit racial biases while explicitly rejecting racial exclusion on the basis of moral reasons such as unfairness and injustice" (Killen et al., 2007). For example, people can easily say that they believe in equal opportunity for all and that they accept all persons, regardless of their skin color or class membership. However, addressing one's own unearned privileges in order to put this statement into practice is much harder than a mere declaration of support. For example, in her study of preservice teachers, King (1991) found that, while most of her students proclaimed disgust with racism, they were quick to defend the status quo and their own privileges, without connecting how those very privileges maintained a racist social order. They exhibited "dysconscious racism," or an uncritical stance toward the existing social order that reinforces White privilege. Pewewardy (1998) describes dysconscious racism as "a form of racism that accepts dominant white norms and privileges" (p. 1). If for example, "you have seen these racial antics and negative behaviors portrayed by Indian mascots . . . hundreds of times, you may become absolutely numb to it" (p. 2). The prevalence of racism normalizes it, and individuals may become numbed to its insidious presence.

I have worked with several people who were excellent at articulating theories and practices about social justice and would speak out against social injustice. They would reach out to marginalized people to support their efforts and stand with them in response to racist or gender biases. However, when they were asked to make a personal sacrifice in order to reduce race and gender biases, they would offer comments similar to the ones that they had spoken against.

A difficult part of program investigation is to determine if the program has staff members who will put the program first instead of themselves. Here we are mostly talking about staff members investing a bit more time, switching teaching assignments, doing community visits, or giving up a seat on a special project in order to have more gender or ethnic representation. Two notable and positive examples come to mind. A year ago, the female students at Thoreau Middle School (pseudonym) displayed a pattern of underachievement in both math and science. The principal wondered if the all-male teaching faculty in those subject areas was serving as a barrier to the girls' achievement. With discussion and negotiation, two of the male teachers decided to transfer from Thoreau to other schools in order to bring in two female math and science teachers. While achievement results were not in as this book went to press—and so we can't "measure" the success of the approach—the point is that these teachers put the students and program first. The second example comes from stories that were told at the celebration of the life of a teacher, Gloria, to whom this book is dedicated. Colleagues and principal said, "She set the bar high for all us. She always arrived at school early, stayed late, visited homes, held high expectation for the students, and demanded that her teacher/friends and colleagues do the same for the ESL [English as a second language] students at the school."

7.1 Take Action

Conduct what I call an "outer role experience." Over the next week, become an observer in your own school.

In the school's office and in the halls, look for evidence of the affirmation of diversity.

Look for how school practices have changed over the past five to ten years (e.g., pictures, posters, school mission, and policy statement).

Who are the students in advanced placement classes?

_____

_____

Who are the students receiving special education services?

_____

_____

What languages and dialects are spoken by the staff?

_____

_____

How aware are students of the historic and present sociopolitical concerns of various social groups? In other words, what sights, sounds, knowledge, and relationships are new to the school once you stop and pay attention?

_____

_____

_____

_____

The diversity that you see is probably greater among the students than anywhere else and is probably a manifestation of both local and global conditions. Paying attention to this diversity, especially its contribution to both local and more global conditions, can inspire innovation and improve our teaching. Answer the questions on pages 80–81 in light of your observations.

THE ACHIEVEMENT REFORM MOVEMENT

According to the U.S. Department of Education's Web site under the section titled "stronger accountability," No Child Left Behind (NCLB) was designed to change the culture of America's schools by closing the achievement gap (http://www.ed.gov/nclb/). Of significant importance—especially to students of color, poor students, and teachers—is that the legislation requires demographic breakouts by subgroups (e.g., special education students, Black students, and others) in order to not hide or, stated more positively, make visible overall group performance. Significant here is that the nonreporting of subgroup performance has allowed U.S. society and policymakers to ignore or tolerate achievement gaps between Whites, and nonwhites and between students living in poverty and middle-class students. According to Lowell C. Rose (2002)—whose article I strongly recommend, "NCLB: Failed Schools—or Failed Law? No Child Left Behind: The Mathematics of Guaranteed Failure."—the following characterizes NCLB as a reform effort:

> *There is much in NCLB to like and embrace. The focus on "leaving no child behind"—systematically identifying and then addressing the needs of low-achieving students—is still a worthy if distant goal. Analyzing test scores, especially those of subgroups, is so basic to improving achievement that it is difficult to understand why its implementation required a federal mandate. . . .*
>
> *The prospects for change depend on many factors, among them political will; the willingness to face the fact that changes are needed; the staying power of those promoting change; and the true motives of those responsible for NCLB—whether they were good intentions marred by haste, disappointment over the results of past legislation, or even a desire to create a stalking-horse for vouchers. If the provisions of NCLB as they stand at this writing are not changed, the greatest consolation for the education community and all concerned may be that the results of NCLB will so lack credibility that they will be not be taken seriously. In that event, NCLB will go down as one of the greatest missed opportunities in the history of American education. (p. 130)*

In addition to Rose's observations, some teachers argue that aspects of U.S. culture, such as a focus on competition and cultural assimilation, must change before the achievement gap can be closed. I believe that both—U.S. and individual school change—must occur simultaneously in order for educational inequity to be eliminated. How and whether educators collectively interpret and react to NCLB and other educational policies will largely determine what change takes place.

The current federal legislation argues for the use of rigorous standards and accountability; it also uses the terms *change* and *innovation*. Reigeluth (1997) writes that there are two uses of standards: "They can be used as tools of standardization—to help make all students alike. Or they can be used as tools for customization—to help meet individual students' needs" (p. 203). Using uniform standards to standardize competes with the idea that students vary greatly in their abilities. Since students have such different abilities, mastery of learning skills, prior knowledge, and home environments, it seems likely that uniform standards will be challenging for some students and easy for others (Riegeluth, 1997). An alternative to using these standards in the classroom in mechanical ways is to use them as tools for customization that help meet students' needs in innovative ways. While I acknowledge that innovation may involve a level of risk that may be greater for some than others, I also believe that reducing the risk of academic failure and helping students to learn will require innovation.

In a classroom, teachers who are aware that their students will face story problems that involve multiplication on a standardized test have several choices. They can drill the students on their multiplication tables, give them sample problems, and then give them feedback on whether their answers are correct or not. Although some students will learn their multiplication tables, complete the problems correctly, and receive positive feedback, other students will not "meet the standard" via this type of teaching and classroom activities. Less innovative teachers, worried that these children will reflect poorly on their skills as teachers, will cajole and even berate these students, stating that they have received all of the instruction that they need to do well and just need to "work harder."

More innovative teachers, less concerned with the risk to themselves than with the well-being of their students, will employ alternative methods that allow students to take different paths to arrive at the same solutions to the problems. These methods may include allowing students to work together in pairs or groups, using CDs that set the multiplication tables to music, teaching one-on-one, assigning a mentor for students (perhaps an older student), meeting and brainstorming with families, and going further to search out the source of the students' academic difficulties. These methods are more time-consuming and require a dedication to putting passion into action.

7.1 Reflection

How have the teachers at your school reacted to the push toward accountability through standardized testing?

_____

_____

_____

Do you think that the federal, state, and/or local legislation and its manifestations will close achievement gaps? Explain your answer.

_____

_____

_____

(Continued)

(Continued)

Many of today's political leaders argue that NCLB should be revised rather than repealed. If you had 10 minutes with the Secretary of Education, what suggestions would you offer for improving the legislation so that it can better work toward closing achievement gaps?

_____

_____

_____

7.2 Take Action

With a teacher/friend, consider the following case study:

Observable information: Ms. Jones teaches fourth grade. She has twenty-two students in her class. She uses balanced literacy methods to ensure that all of her students are able to read and write on grade level, and most of her students' test scores reflect that her methods are effective. However, one student, Jack, a Chinese-American boy with low self-esteem in the classroom, has struggled with his reading and math test scores. Jack defies the model minority stereotype; he rarely completes his homework and is always underperforming relative to his classmates. Over the past semester, other teachers have become frustrated with Jack's performance because it is not consistent with their expectations of what he can and should do. He is regarded as a low-achieving student.

Jack's mother is single and works two jobs. He often takes care of his two younger siblings after school, which includes feeding them and putting them to bed. Ms. Jones reasons that Jack's mother is not concerned about his education because several attempts to reach her have failed. In addition, Jack often comes to school sleepy and is becoming increasingly disconnected from his school work. Furthermore, Ms. Jones has noticed that some of his Asian American friends are no longer spending time with Jack. Ms. Jones concludes that her methods work for most students and that Jack may just be one of those students who "won't make it."

Information waiting to be discovered: Jack does not see a connection to his life with the literature selections he is asked to read. He has a bright mind but is weighed down with the concerns of his home life. He understands that his support of his family is essential but also at times feels frustrated and overwhelmed. In addition, he does not see schooling as a path to changing his life circumstances.

What to do: Instead of giving up on Jack, what could Ms. Jones do to reconnect Jack with academic achievement, bolster his confidence, and show support for his completion of responsibilities at home? Create a plan by listing strategies, instructional methods, and resources that she could use. Describe the attitude you would suggest that she adopt toward Jack. Be sure to consider the following items:

- Resources in the community
- Mentoring ideas
- Help with understanding varying communication styles
- An exploration of Jack's extracurricular interests
- Rapport building
- Support from other staff members and Jack's mother

Action Plan 7: Program Investigation

This week I encourage you to become an observer in your own school. Now try to consider how the school looks and feels to a parent who either doesn't, for example, speak English or is disabled. To make this more authentic, survey the parents in your class. You may choose to ask them some of the questions on pages 80–81. List the major ideas that struck you from the survey here:

_____

_____

_____

_____

While you may not be able to redesign the whole school's climate this week (although some of you certainly may be able to!), list ways that you can make your own classroom more welcoming and fruitful for the children and families you serve.

_____

_____

_____

_____

Ask parents for literature recommendations to include in your classroom library or to contribute ideas for artwork or artifacts. The possibilities are endless.

8 Implementing Change

Step 4

KNOWLEDGE BASE FOR
CLOSING THE ACHIEVEMENT GAPS

Much of the educational research over the past 30 years has focused on what makes teachers effective. Although this research continues, the focus is more inclusive. Now at issue is what it takes to be an effective teacher with students who are not experiencing academic success or who are bored with or disengaged from school. This focus is particularly common in studies on students of color and students who live in urban and rural areas that are characterized by high levels of poverty. The educational literature—as well as the experiences of teachers who are effective with all children, regardless of their academic ability, ethnicity, socioeconomic status, family structure, and/or English-speaking ability—continually tells me that attention must be given to teachers' knowledge, skills, and attitudes. In other words, deep content knowledge is only one dimension of efficacy that teachers exhibit in the classroom. Other dimensions include attitudes—in particular, attitudes about valuing all students and affirming diversity.

Movement from the investigating phase to the implementing phase features the establishment of new routines and different ways of viewing old orientations. In short, it involves enacting the knowledge and skills learned during the investigating phase and displaying comfort with and an optimism about the ongoing change/transition process. Much that is written here about implementing change to eliminate achievement gaps and affirm diversity includes variations of ideas you may have heard before. However, the information is presented here in a way that hopefully will inspire you to move toward a different interpretation of the possibilities for change in your classroom and school. Below, in Did You Know 8.1, is a chart adapted from the work of Ladson-Billings (1994) to remind you of and help you focus on the knowledge, skills, and disposition that are culturally relevant as you implement change.

? 8.1 Did You Know?

Culturally relevant	*Assimilationist*
Knowledge is continuously recreated, recycled, and shared by teachers and students. It is not static or unchanging.	Knowledge is static and is passed in one direction, from teacher to student.
Knowledge is viewed critically.	Knowledge is viewed as infallible.
Teacher is passionate about content.	Teacher is detached, neutral about content.
Teacher helps students develop necessary skills.	Teacher expects students to demonstrate prerequisite skills.
Teacher sees excellence as a complex standard that may involve some postulates but takes student diversity and individual differences into account.	Teacher sees excellence as a postulate that exists independently from student diversity or individual differences.

KNOWLEDGE OF CURRICULAR CONTENT: A STRONG SUBJECT MATTER BASE

Most teachers agree that having a strong knowledge base is crucial. As Connelly, Clandinin, and He (1997) state,

> *Teacher knowledge and knowing affects every aspect of the teaching act. It affects teachers' relationships with students; teachers' interpretations of subject matter and its importance in students' lives; teachers' treatment of ideas whether as fixed textbook given or as matter of inquiry and reflection; teachers'*

*curriculum planning and evaluation of students' progress; and so on. In short,
it has . . . become commonplace to believe that what teachers know and how
they express their knowledge is central to student learning. (p. 666)*

During the past two decades, educators have steadfastly urged
teachers to acquire in-depth content knowledge. In order to bolster the
importance of a strong subject matter base for teachers, No Child Left
Behind (NCLB) enforced the standard of "highly qualified" teachers.
Under Title I, a highly qualified teacher meets the following conditions:

- Holds a minimum of a bachelor's degree;
- Has obtained full state certification or licensure;
- Has demonstrated subject area competence in each of the academic
  subjects in which the teacher teaches;
- Has, as a new elementary teacher, passed a rigorous state test that
  demonstrates competence in subject matter and teaching skills in
  reading, writing, mathematics, and the other areas of the basic elementary school curriculum;
- Has, as a new secondary teacher, passed a rigorous state examination in the content areas in which he or she is certified.
- Has taken general education tests that assess knowledge about,
  for example, developmental psychology and theories of classroom
  management.

KNOWLEDGE ABOUT TEACHING: PEDAGOGICAL CONTENT KNOWLEDGE

There is unanimity among educators that teachers who are working to close
the achievement gap must know their subject matter. But to be able to teach
the subject matter, a teacher must also know what makes a topic difficult or
easy for students and be able to "unpack" the conceptual underpinnings of
the subject matter for their class. If you believe that good teaching is a skill,
you are correct; good teaching includes an understanding of the organization, presentation, and *content* of the subject matter. Thus, pedagogical content knowledge denotes a teacher's ability to organize and present subject
matter in ways that makes it understandable to and applicable by students.

John Dewey (1977) argued that teachers must be able to "psychologize"
the subject matter for students. Dewey meant that the teacher has to consider the nature of the subject matter, its application to the real world, and
its connection to the students. Teachers who are teaching to close achievement gaps take concepts apart, place them in a real-world context central to
the lives of students, and challenge them by developing inquiry-based
lessons. An excellent example of this "psychologizing" of subject matter is

found in the teaching of Brian Schultz. Schultz (2008), a fifth-grade teacher in Chicago, demonstrates how to make this happen. He challenged students from a housing project to identify a problem in their community that they wanted to solve. The students unanimously chose as their problem the replacement of their dilapidated school building, which they devoted a class project to and repeatedly presented public arguments about. The students started by reporting that, in their school, there was no lunchroom, horrible toilet facilities, broken windows, windows with bullet holes, a poorly stocked library, an absence of computers, and poorly heated classrooms. They then examined how, and argued that they were, disenfranchised from society and from the right to a healthy and safe educational environment. As the students prepared their argument for the replacement of their school, they also developed a new curriculum that included expository and persuasive writing, interviews, and the development and conducting of surveys. Other project activities included mathematics, such as computing and analyzing survey results; public speaking, such as giving interviews with local television stations and news reporters; developing and giving talks to raise funds for their project; and developing listening skills, such as when receiving advice from Ralph Nader and local and state politicians.

The result of the students' efforts did not lead to a new school, but it did lead to a great deal of academic success and civic and social respectability—the students' test scores greatly improved; they met and exceeded state standards; several of the students, along with their teacher, presented the class curriculum project at several education conferences, including the American Education Research Association (AERA) annual meeting; and class members appeared on television and held meetings with State of Illinois and City of Chicago officials.

PEDAGOGICAL SKILLS FOR CLOSING THE ACHIEVEMENT GAPS

The science of teaching may lie in the content, but the art of teaching lies in the delivery of that content. Grossman, McDonald, Hammerness, and Ronfeldt (2008) see skilled performance as revolving around a set of procedures that include knowing what to do, when to do it, and how to do it effectively. Teachers who have success with closing achievement gaps agree with Grossman et al. They know procedures that allow them to teach in varied ways, communicate effectively with students, manage the classroom successfully, and use technology as a tool for more advanced learning. In addition, having pedagogical skills means that teachers have not only a knowledge base that is derived from multiple funds of knowledge (e.g., traditional texts, the students' neighborhood and family experiences), they have the ability to make it accessible and engaging to students.

As classrooms undergo demographic changes, teachers' pedagogical skills cannot remain static; they must be constantly evolving. To return to an earlier point, today's students live in a globalized society and need to be taught accordingly. Students raised in the "culture of power," particularly a class of more privileged students, can learn to develop identities that are not based on gaining power over others, and this can be done in many ways in a classroom. Students can learn to consider the perspectives and experiences of others through contact with those different from themselves, especially if they are working cooperatively with partners from other schools and/or community members toward a particular outcome (e.g., advocating for a cause in which they believe). In addition, students can learn to consider their own actions responsibly and understand that acting in their self-interest alone often means acting against someone else's best interest.

Think about the extent to which the following statements in the Teacher Pedagogical Skill Survey, based on Beaudin and Hadden (2004), apply to you. Cite examples of how you already do the things listed in the statements. If you find yourself lacking in certain areas, think about how you can develop your skills in those areas. Discuss with a teacher/friend how you can develop your pedagogical skills.

TEACHER PEDAGOGICAL SKILLS SURVEY

1. I am able to incorporate various teaching styles, course materials, and lesson plans that benefit all of my students. I understand the limitations of using only one instructional method and that teaching styles and approaches may be culture bound. When I am unable to provide appropriate instruction, I take the appropriate steps, which may include consultation, supervision, and coteaching. Furthermore, I continuously seek to further my skills by seeking consultation, supervision, and continuing education.

    Always   Sometimes   Rarely

2. I am able to implement various forms of assessment within my classroom, in ways that will allow the students from various backgrounds to thrive in their education. I use both individualistic and collectivistic evaluation tools.

    Always   Sometimes   Rarely

3. I attend and work to eliminate biases, prejudices, and discriminatory practices within the education system. I am cognizant of sociopolitical contexts in conducting evaluations and providing education and am developing sensitivity to issues of oppression, sexism, elitism, and racism. I am a social activist on behalf of my students and their families.

    Always   Sometimes   Rarely

REFLECTIVE SKILLS

Developing reflective skills or the ability to analyze and act on teacher-generated data does not mean thinking only about what is happening in the classroom. Instead, this process entails studying your classroom practice in order to make changes that will result in a more democratic, ethical, and student-centered classroom where learning takes place every minute of the day (Zeichner & Liston, 1996). Some teachers erroneously believe that if they spend time thinking about their teaching then they are being reflective. For example, Nancy, a teacher I know, was experiencing anxiety over writing students' names on the board and placing check marks after them to indicate each instance of the students' misbehavior. Nancy noticed that she was writing the names of Native American students on the board or adding checkmarks to Native American names. She thought and thought about what she was doing but did little to understand how she was determining whose name to write, how the classroom dynamics contributed to the behavior of the students, or how her own ideas about appropriate and inappropriate behavior were based on her experiences as a person with a particular class, racial, ethnic, and religious background.

Nancy's case demonstrates that instruction and curriculum need to be connected. To make this connection more seamless, Dewey (1977) encouraged teachers to act in the following manner:

> *Abandon the notion of subject matter [curriculum] as something fixed and readymade in itself, outside the child's experience; cease thinking of the child as also something hard and fast; see it as something fluent, embryonic, vital: and we realize that the child and curriculum are simply two limits which define a single process. (p. 19)*

In addition, Dewey claimed that, just as there is a difference between learning about the land from a map and learning firsthand from the journey itself, there is also a difference between learning about fractions from a text versus learning about them through experimentation under the patient guidance of a teacher. The latter learning experience should be connected to and derived from the students' own experiences to make it more meaningful. For example, I am teaching fractions to my six-year-old granddaughter, Amaya, by way of baking cakes. Over the past year, Amaya and I frequently get together to bake a cake. She selects the cake she wants us to bake from looking at pictures of cakes in my cookbooks. Presently, she is doing most of the measuring, mixing, and cleaning up. By using several different measuring tools, she has learned to add and subtract fractions and, more importantly, how to bake a delicious cake.

8.1 Reflection

What could Nancy do to investigate the act of writing students' names on the board, including the reasons and outcomes from the perspective of the students and the teacher?

_____

_____

_____

8.2 Reflection

What efforts have you made recently to teach students about the ways of working in mainstream society?

_____

_____

_____

For example, I sometimes see students, especially students of color, wearing their coat and hat in the classroom throughout the day. To my eyes, they look uncomfortable or like they are anxiously waiting to leave the classroom and school. Adopting such behavior when applying for a job or attending an event where hats and coats are usually taken off can cause the students to be looked upon as not belonging there, not understanding the code of conduct. I have started to develop a collection of articles and pictures that address clothing, grooming, behavior, and action in formal and informal settings. I give these resources to students to help them better understand the habits and customs of mainstream society. In addition, I am mindful of the teaching of Lisa Delpit (1996) when she argues that it is not enough just to insist on adherence to the culture of power; so I also include in the collection a critique of traditional middle class behavior and that helps students to appreciate and understand the value of their own culture and behavior.

Action Plan 8: Teacher Knowledge About Content and Pedagogy

I. This week, I encourage you to humbly admit that one person can never know everything there is to know, even about their main subject matter. However, we can partner with others, making us stronger and more knowledgeable through these partnerships. We can also seek ways to constantly expand and improve our knowledge in the areas that affect who we are as people and what we can bring to the classroom. As a teacher, any new experiences you gain or knowledge you discover will benefit your students. In the Take Action section, we encouraged you to team up with someone to discuss a classroom lesson or practice that you already do. Identify, recommend changes, and make a list of some changes you plan on making to this lesson or strategy:

_____

_____

_____

II. Next, plan on doing something to expand your knowledge and experience this week. It can be something you do immediately. Think about your own interests. What activities feed your soul? Can you find a cooking class to take this week? How about joining a local running group and training for a race? You could join a book club at a local library to meet others not involved in the field of education. Describe your plan:

_____

_____

_____

_____

III. Now, plan on a specific activity to increase your content knowledge or pedagogical skill in the classroom. Is there a travel grant for which you could apply to enhance your teaching about a specific country or geographic region? How about a class at the local university? (Pick one that you are interested in, not one that you need for recertification.)

Is there a conference you have "been meaning" to attend in your subject matter or area of interest but have not found the time? Enroll in it this week. Ask your principal how you can find funds or pay for it yourself. Remember, this is about enriching your own knowledge as well as that of your students. You will absolutely be able to apply this new knowledge in your classroom. Anything that you do to expand your own horizons will also expand those of your students! List your ideas here:

_____

_____

_____

IV. Also this week, I encourage you to explore how societal structures have a negative effect on the perceived achievement of some of your students. Delve into this by reading a book about the experiences of minority cultures in society and in schools. Choose the same book as a teacher/friend, so that you can hold each other accountable and have someone with whom to discuss the book. Take a trip to the local bookstore. Find any book that speaks to your interests on the oppression of minority groups in American education. Some recommendations would be anything by Jonathan Kozol, *36 Children*, by Herb Kohl, *The Autobiography of Malcolm X, Other People's Children*, by Lisa Delpit, *Dreamkeepers*, by Gloria Ladson-Billings, *Teaching to Transgress*, by bell hooks, or *The Marginalized Minds of Black Men*, by Alford Young. Keep track of the ways in which your mind is opened to the diverse experiences of people in America while reading.

You may notice that some minority groups have less attention paid to their struggles. Therefore, looking at documentaries or movies from Web sites focusing on cultural criticism, anti-oppression, or human rights might provide resources. If you like old movies, I have good one for you: *Gentleman's Agreement*, a semi-love story about a journalist who crusades against anti-Semitism in the 1940s, starring Gregory Peck and Dorothy McGuire.

Additionally, resources that speak to cross-group alliances or social justice activism from the perspective of those in dominant and privileged groups (e.g., Time Wise's *White Like Me*; James McBride's *The Color of the Water*) can be eye-opening and informative; and helpful for developing ways to eliminate oppression and privilege in the school and the larger society.

Part III

Change/Solutions in Practice

This section differs from the previous sections by more directly dealing with teacher-student engagement. I begin with a discussion in Chapter 8 of knowledge and skills needed to close the achievement gap; this is followed in Chapter 9 with a discussion of how to make schools placed where students can have significant achievements.

9 Cultural Competence

GOAL 1: MAKING SCHOOLS PLACES WHERE STUDENTS CAN HAVE SIGNIFICANT ACHIEVEMENTS

A. High Student Interest

When students make the decision to pursue an instructional goal, it influences the quality of their learning (Collopy & Green, 1995). In addition, when instructional goals are defined by students' quest for knowledge rather than their ability, as measured by standardized tests or other assessments, students are more likely to remain interested in the idea and to develop a deeper knowledge base. In many instances, the joy of learning causes students to exceed the learning expectations teachers have of them and brings out students' true learning capabilities. Therefore, it is important that teachers analyze what is understood by "learning capabilities." Learning means not simply assimilating knowledge but actually producing it. As Gloria Ladson-Billings (1994) states:

> Scholars have come to recognize knowledge as a social construction. But, unfortunately, the 'school knowledge' that most students experience is offered up as a given. The role and responsibility of students are merely to accept that given and reproduce it via recitation or writing. Even with the clamor for more critical thinking, memory continues to be the most rewarded skill in the nation's classrooms. But culturally relevant teaching attempts to help students understand and participate in knowledge-building. (p. 81)

Schools should be places where students can have access to learning that engages them, not only so that they enjoy it, but also because engaged students persist in completing their work despite learning challenges and obstacles. Such engagement is linked to four instructional goals: success, curiosity, originality, and satisfying relationships (Strong, Silver, & Robinson, 1995). Success is the desire for mastery; curiosity is the desire for understanding; originality is the desire for self-expression; and satisfying relationships are the desire for involvement with others. I observed the achievement of all four desires when recently attending the finals for a poetry slam. During the poetry slam, students were passionately demonstrating many of the academic concepts taught in literacy, social studies, music, and drama. Along with demonstrating the academic concepts, they were also critically analyzing and challenging ways of negative thinking that are implicit not only in textbooks but also in society at large, such as the role of women in society, the inequitable treatment of women, or the use of stereotypical language to characterize people within marginalized groups. The poetry slammers, in their message, described good and caring teaching as well as teachers whose subject matter knowledge, skills, and disposition met their needs and interests. Take Action 9.1 can serve as a rubric to help teachers assess their conceptions of their knowledge base.

9.1 Take Action

"Conceptions of Knowledge" from Ladson-Billings (1994)

Analyze the "Conceptions of Knowledge" chart. Choose a subject area that you teach, and list a strategy to help you accomplish each statement on the culturally relevant side of the chart.

Culturally Relevant	Assimilationist	Subject Area	Strategy
Knowledge is continuously recreated, recycled, and shared by teachers and students. It is not static or unchanging.	Knowledge is static and is passed in one direction, from teacher to student.		
Knowledge is viewed critically.	Knowledge is viewed as infallible.		
Teacher is passionate about content.	Teacher is detached, neutral about content.		

(Continued)

(Continued)

Culturally Relevant	Assimilationist	Subject Area	Strategy
Teacher helps students develop necessary skills.	Teacher expects students to demonstrate prerequisite skills.		
Teacher sees excellence as a complex standard that may involve some postulates but takes student diversity and individual differences into account.	Teacher sees excellence as a postulate that exists independently from student diversity or individual differences.		

B. Culturally Relevant Curriculum

Culturally relevant teaching takes place when the curriculum content is connected to the students' cultural background and teachers' instruction takes advantage of this connection. This connection allows students to develop their true learning capabilities. Culturally relevant teaching is effective in both monocultural and multicultural classrooms, as well as in classrooms where students speak a language other than English, have disabilities, or have not had the kinds of social experiences at home that advantage them at school. Ladson-Billings (1994) explains that culturally relevant teaching is engaging for students because using their culture and history in instruction help maintain that culture and transcend the negative effects of the dominant culture. Such was the case at the poetry slam I noted above. The poetry included students' presentation of classroom assignments representing different subject areas and their thinking about the relevance (or lack of relevance) of the assignment to their lives. Also, there were comments about the schooling they were receiving and in some cases the schools themselves. In addition, some poets spoke of their life outside of school, including family members, their life circumstances, and life chances. The poets were not nasty or demeaning about schools or teachers, but they were frank and realistic.

Gay (1975) observes that culturally relevant teaching is engaging because it is comprehensive and inclusive. She states, "Fragmented and isolated units, courses, and bits of information about ethnic groups interspersed sporadically into the school curriculum and instructional program will not do the job. . . . Nor will additive approaches, wherein school curriculum remains basically the same, and ethnic content becomes an appendage" (p. 178). Instead, when teaching poetry, one should use poetry written by members of different ethnic groups, both in the United States and abroad, and integrate multicultural poems into the different poetry genres that one teaches. This approach not only teaches students that individuals from different groups have written poetry; it also enriches students' understanding of this art form by enabling students to explore how diverse ethnic groups have contributed to the various poetic forms under study.

In culturally relevant teaching, teachers strive to use the contributions and perspectives of the group to depict each group as it would depict itself (Sleeter & Grant, 2007). This teaching should also show those aspects of the group's culture that are important to its members. Sleeter and Grant explain this point with the following example:

> Teachers wishing to include American Indians in the curriculum sometimes choose Sacagawea as a heroine to discuss; but from many American Indian perspectives, Sequoyah would be a preferable historical figure. Sacagawea served dominant group interests by leading Lewis and Clark west, whereas Sequoyah served the interests of the Cherokee by developing an alphabet for encoding the Cherokee language. (p. 178)

Note that this approach does not mean changing the topic of study (Native Americans). It does involve becoming informed about the differing perspectives and experiences involved and changing teaching plans accordingly.

Promoting a space where students can engage in the production of knowledge requires that their history, background, and culture be taken into account when planning lessons. School should not require that children negate their cultural identities, for example, by asking students to forsake their home language (including not only foreign languages but also Black English/Ebonics) in order to learn standardized English. That said, a culturally relevant curriculum does not ignore the skills and knowledge that will enable the students to gain access to the culture of power. Knowledge of mainstream society and knowledge of the skills needed to succeed in mainstream society will help students to be productive in other academic settings, workplaces, and social institutions. Schools have the complex burden and teachers have the harder work of helping children maintain their identities while developing the necessary skills they need to succeed in school and beyond. Sharroky Hollie's work—the books *Talkin' Black Talk* and *The Skin That We Speak*, as well as the DVD *Culture and Language Academy of Success*—are excellent resources for accomplishing this.

C. Creating Culturally Responsive Classrooms

Andrade and Hakim (1995) contend that student involvement and leadership are essential to their becoming instructionally engaged. They say that by involving their first-grade students in instruction and allowing them to make decisions about it, "We now see learning through a much more powerful lens, viewing the whole child in relation to his or her prior knowledge and dominant language and culture. The more we look, the more we see" (p. 23). Their words suggest a kind of culturally responsive teaching that helps to affirm diversity, our second goal, by creating a caring space with a social-emotional climate that supports the needs of all members of the learning community.

Much of Withhall's (1949) research on classroom climate is supported by current research (e.g., Kumar, 2007). Withhall argued that the climate of the classroom influences (1) the private world of the students, (2) the "esprit de corps" of the class, (3) the sense of purpose and relevance to group and individual goals and activities, (4) the ability to look at problems objectively, and (5) the strength of student-teacher and student-student rapport. Similarly Kumar (2007) states "The classroom climate influences the student achievement, their self-esteem and participation in the lesson. The most important aspect of classroom climate is the relationship between teacher and students. There must be elements of caring, trust, and respect in the interpersonal relationships between teachers and students" (p. 1). In other words, instructional engagement demands a classroom environment in which every student comes to believe, "I count, I care, and I can" (Dodd, 1995, p. 66). To establish a classroom climate that is responsive to the diversity of students' backgrounds in the classroom, teachers need to consider four motivational conditions:

1. *Establishing inclusion*—creating a caring learning community where respect is established between teacher and students as well as among the students themselves;

2. *Developing attitude*—teacher and students deciding upon learning experiences that both believe are important to students' achievement and life circumstances;

3. *Enhancing meaning*—providing challenging, relevant learning experiences that teach students how to have greater control over their life circumstances; and

4. *Engendering competence*—understanding that all students are academically curious and should be expected to learn. (Wlodkowski & Ginsberg, 1995, p. 17)

Wlodkowski and Ginsberg (1995) claim that these four conditions work together to influence teacher and student behaviors and attitudes.

9.1 Reflection

Harold, a teacher planning to implement Wlodkowski and Ginsberg's (1995) four conditions, said to me, "Here is my summary statement of their ideas. Do I have it?"

It is the belief that every student can learn and treating them so leads to positive relationships between teachers and students, which in turn fosters a classroom climate where students look forward to challenging learning experiences, which helps them to have control over their life circumstances.

What do you think? Does Harold "have it?"

_____

_____

Write your summary statement?

_____

_____

_____

9.1 Do You Know?

Student Engagement

Working with middle school students, Wasserstein (1995) identified five maxims that teachers can use to help students become engaged:

1. All students need to see the link between routine drill and practice and more complex work. Many teachers will eliminate any memorization at all in the classroom, while often it can be valuable to directly teach skills and information if it can be linked to authentic learning.

2. Students need to tinker with real-world problems, and they need opportunities to construct knowledge.

3. The "basics" should not be an end in themselves but a means to an end.

(Continued)

(Continued)

4. Teachers need to nurture a strong self-image by allowing students to develop an internal locus of control, and to be aware of their strengths and weaknesses.

5. Self-esteem is enhanced when students accomplish something they thought impossible, something beyond them.

9.2 Reflection

Keeping Wasserstein's (1995) five maxims in mind, identify two students in your class who will benefit from your application of this work.

_____

_____

D. Promoting Gender-Responsive Classrooms

Developing gender equity is central to closing achievement gaps and affirming diversity. This is especially so in the areas of science and mathematics, subjects in which males are assumed to naturally excel over females until not too long ago (and still today in some situations—even former Harvard President Lawrence Summers suggested that innate differences between men and women might be the source of differences in gender representation in math and science). An early response to gender inequity was to teach girls to "act more like boys": to be more aggressive, tough, and competitive. However, this approach has not met with much success. It suggested that acting in a male way was "normal," thereby positioning "girl's/women's ways" in opposition to the "norm." This way of thinking about gender differences, for example, helped to create the unequal representation of men and women in leadership positions and disparate compensation for male and female employees.

To address these inequities, Pollina (1995) suggests using a feminist approach when teaching math and science. By a feminist approach, Pollina means that teachers should encourage all students to question "facts" and beliefs that frame high-status work and notions of success, which have historically been associated with men and masculinity, as normal. Although Pollina's suggestions specifically focus on math and science instruction, they can be applied to make teaching gender responsive in all subject areas:

- Connect mathematics, science, and technology to the real world.
- Choose metaphors carefully or have students develop their own so that they do not only take into account boys' life experiences.
- Foster true collaboration. Pulling desks into circles does not ensure a collaborative, noncompetitive experience. True collaboration requires that students are engaged in an authentic group task that cannot be solved alone and that requires positive interdependence (everyone depends on everyone else to complete the task), individual accountability (there is a system for grading/assessing each individual's understanding and contribution), equal participation (each person's role is of equal importance), and simultaneous interaction (everyone participates at the same time). (See Cohen & Lotan, 1997; Kagan, 1985.)
- Encourage girls to act as experts. Only when a student group is responsible for verifying its own logic and when students critique their own work and that of their peers do they begin to see themselves as scientists.
- Give girls the opportunity to be in control of technology.
- Portray technology not only as a form of entertainment but as a way to solve problems as well.
- Capitalize on students' verbal and writing strengths. For example, Pollina's (1995) calculus students keep journals in which they reflect on their experiences in her class, comment on their progress, and set goals for themselves. Two possible journal prompts are these:
  - You died while doing your physics homework. Write your physics obituary.
  - You are a spider on the wall of your room observing yourself doing your mathematics homework. What do you see?
- Experiment with testing and evaluation. Assessment methods must reflect the research suggesting that many girls do not think in linear right/wrong categories.
- Give frequent feedback and keep expectations high. Because girls still may not expect to do well in mathematics and science, they tend to need more encouragement than do boys.

E. Knowledge of the Community

Teachers' knowledge of the community where they work is becoming increasingly complicated and challenging. At some schools, many of the students come from distant locations; some ride a bus to school for more than 30 minutes. In addition, as we continue to note, population demographics are changing and making schools more diverse. To get an assessment about your knowledge of the school community, complete the Teacher Knowledge of Community/Diversity Statement and Reflection 9.3.

TEACHER KNOWLEDGE OF COMMUNITY/DIVERSITY SURVEY

1. I possess specific knowledge and information about the particular groups with which I am working. I am aware of the cultural heritages and historical backgrounds of my culturally different students. I understand that a superficial knowledge of other cultures may further my stereotyping, and therefore, I seek an in-depth knowledge of other cultures, beliefs, values, and lifestyles.

   I agree   I agree somewhat   I disagree

2. I understand how variables such as culture, race/ethnicity, sexual orientation, gender, and so forth may affect the educational processes (i.e., learning styles, educational choices, the identification of learning disorders, relationships with teachers, elders, and authority figures, help-seeking behavior, etc.). Furthermore, I am able to apply information from various racial, ethnic, gender, and sexual orientation identity development models to assist in my understanding of my relationships and communications with individual students. Educators can take such variables into account when determining a variety of teaching approaches.

   I agree   I agree somewhat   I disagree

3. I understand and have knowledge of sociopolitical influences that impinge on the life of minorities. Immigration issues, poverty, racism, stereotyping, institutional barriers, and powerlessness all leave major scars that may influence the education and social development process.

   I agree   I agree somewhat   I disagree

4. I value differences in communication styles, including bilingualism, and view them as assets to education. I recognize the challenges that students may face within our education system when English is not the native language. I encourage all my students to develop bilingual skills, and I work to improve my own bilingual competence.

   I agree   I agree somewhat   I disagree

5. I am aware that various forms of testing and assessment may be culture and class bound and therefore may place certain students at a disadvantage. I attempt to ameliorate the negative impact of standardized testing by creating varied forms of testing and evaluation within my classroom. Furthermore, I recognize the large-scale effects of biased assessment, such as overrepresentation of minorities in special education and lower level tracks.

   I agree   I agree somewhat   I disagree

6. I have knowledge and respect for minority family structures, hier-archies, values, and beliefs. I am knowledgeable about the community characteristics and the resources in the community, as well as the family. I understand how this may affect my students and how I communicate with them and their families. I understand the great heterogeneity existing within cultural groups.

    I agree   I agree somewhat   I disagree

7. I understand that being a multicultural teacher must be pervasive through all facets of my professional work. It extends to all of my students, the faculty with whom I work, my lesson plans, my classroom environment, and so forth to create a more open place for students from various backgrounds to strive. On a personal level, I strive to develop a multicultural personality.

    I agree   I agree somewhat   I disagree

9.3 Reflection

Closely examine one of the above statements above with a teacher/friend. Remember, if you are a White teacher, some (who may also be members of your racial group) say White people are often unaware of racial injustices and oppression that occur for people of racial minority groups. The same is said of other categories associated with dominant and privileged groups in which individuals identify as members. Consider how your roles and identities affect your responses.

Create strategies to further develop your knowledge in the area described by the statement you have chosen. For example, if you have chosen Number 5 but don't understand how forms of tests can place students from certain cultures and classes at a disadvantage, research this. Read a book or article by Lisa Delpit, bell hooks, Geneva Gay, or Sonia Nieto. Survey a variety of people about their experiences with standardized tests. Look at the stories and questions on a standardized test. Consider how the background knowledge and experiences of the White middle class are favored in answering these questions. Ask children to process their responses to certain questions aloud so you can observe their thought processes as they answer the questions.

Action Plan 9: Cultural Competence and Culturally Relevant Teaching

This week choose a subject area you teach and design strategies that demonstrate your cultural competence and your ability to do culturally relevant teaching. Provided are five questions dealing with the conceptions of knowledge. Here we present space for your ideas. List a strategy to help you accomplish each of the following:

1. How can you display the truth that knowledge is continuously recreated, recycled, and shared by teachers and students rather than static and unchanging?

   _____

   _____

   _____

2. How can you encourage your students to view knowledge critically?

   _____

   _____

   _____

3. How can you become passionate about the content you teach in your lessons?

   _____

   _____

   _____

4. How can you help your students develop the necessary skills they will need to learn?

   _____

   _____

   _____

5. How can you continue to view excellence in your classroom as a complex standard that may involve some postulates (standards) but take student diversity and individual differences into account?

_____

_____

_____

Also, this week, I am asking you to expand your cultural competence in order to increase your culturally relevant teaching by attending community events that your students attend and also by examining the historical construction of your specific subject area. Here, we ask you to apply this experience and information to your classroom by encouraging your students to excel in and value their home cultures' traditions. Remember that this will not take away from the "mainstream" skills that standardized tests measure. Be sure to bring all of these values and traditions into contact with all of your students. The understanding and globalized attitudes in your classroom will be exponentially enhanced.

At the end of the week list the cultural competences you expanded:

_____

_____

_____

10 Change/ Solutions in Practice

Four Examples

I t would be great if I could visit your school and spend time talking with you and your colleagues before offering to you these four examples, expanded on from Grant (2007) Sleeter and, that cover primary, elementary, middle, and high school; however, since you can't "beam me over," we will have to go with the next best thing. The first example, "Story Time," is framed around the teaching of reading at the elementary level. A lesson plan format is used to structure my discussion; however, prior to the lesson plan, I contextualize putting the change into practice. In presenting the examples, I am assuming that you and your teacher/friends have completed the reading and activities (e.g., Reflections, Take Action) on the achievement gaps, diversity, power, and change/transition throughout this book. In addition, you have completed most—hopefully all—of the end-of-the-chapter activities. Now, you are probably saying, "OK, Carl, com'on. Get on with it." So away we go.

EXAMPLE I

Bring together your colleagues who teach at the elementary level and share with them that you plan to take action in dealing with the achievement gaps and diversity. Point out to them that your ideas are not extraneous and irrelevant to state standards and curriculum demands but are in keeping with 21st-century demands. Acknowledge that you understand their fears and concern about not strictly adhering to the district-imposed curricula, but they must speak truth and take actions that will best benefit their students. Critically significant, explain to them that the "deviation" from the prescribed curriculum will not produce lower test scores or threaten their jobs but will instead help students to become more engaged and make their jobs as teachers more fulfilling. Next, explain to them how you are implementing change.

Begin by reminding your colleagues that many—if not most—students who enter school with what is termed school knowledge do well from the start, especially in reading. Students who enter school without this knowledge are often members of an oppressed group, and many times they are of the "low-reading group" or characterized as "corrective readers." Once behind, they tend to fall farther below their grade levels. Point out that the research and best practice literature argues that teachers' words and actions can greatly influence students, so both their attitude and behavior must suggest to the low-reading group students that, with hard work, they can improve. Tell your colleagues that one way to engage students in reading is to have them help you set up the reading centers. Remind them that if they set up the center alone, it is only another teaching tool. Yes, the students may say, "Wow!" "Great!" or "Look at all of the wonderful books!" when they enter the room the following morning, but is it really their center? They didn't work for it, help in the selection of books, or loan their favorite book to the center. In addition, tell your teacher/friends that you are going to give the students more freedom/responsibility by encouraging them to take charge of literature circle discussions as soon as they feel ready.

Tell your colleagues that, just as the nation remains on a terror alert, the class will remain on a respect-all-people-and-look-out-for-bias alert. Smith, Greenlaw, and Scott (1987) discovered that many books most often read in elementary classrooms have stereotypic sex roles and are devoid of people of color and those with mental or physical disabilities. Similarly, Smith et al. (1987) confirm this view and argue that such biases have a detrimental effect on children of color and foster a biased view of a world that is becoming increasingly interdependent. Both authors are implicitly arguing that the books in the reading center should offer a more equitable view of society while tapping the experiential background of a wide range of students. A book that you can suggest to your teacher/friends that will help them with the selection of books and one that their students can use is, *Beyond Heroes and Holidays*, edited by Lee, Menkart and Okazawa-Rey (1998). This publication contains numerous articles on how to help students detect bias in books, videos, software, and the media.

Tell your colleagues you plan to work on reading skills (e.g., comprehension, inferences) demanded by the state standards through proposing critical questions related to acts of justice and injustice that the students read about in the books. Point out that the use of books is a nonthreatening way for students to ask questions related to oppression. By using the story's plot and characters, you can develop issues of social inequity outside students' own lives. As students feel comfortable with the issues, you will gradually lead the discussion to the lives of the students. As children begin to recognize incidents involving oppression in their own lives, they can see these incidents in context rather than as a personal statement about themselves.

State that your teaching will be interdisciplinary. Growing out of students' reading, individual students, the class as a whole, or small groups will be instructed to design a project that includes at least three subject areas. Through a collective process of choosing a follow-up project, either as a class or in small groups and with you as guide, students learn to choose among alternatives in a manner that is fair to all participants (e.g., you may draw on cooperative learning structures such as "Numbered Heads Together" or "Spend a Buck" to teach cooperative learning; see Kagan, 1985). By sharing projects, students become aware of alternative methods for goal accomplishment and gain an appreciation of the learning styles of their peers.

Tell your teacher/friends that follow-up activities will be included. Whether suggested by you or students, they will require students to apply what they have learned to another situation. For many students, the ideas will be new and may need to be further thought out and assimilated. Some students may benefit from a project that opens avenues for discussion with others. A purpose of the plan is to place students in the active roles of critical thinkers and problem solvers as they consider conditions that structure equality and inequality. Thus, the reading becomes not only exciting and enjoyable to students but a communicative and human relations process among students as well. When reading reaches this level, students use it to take advantage of opportunities and to generate workable alternatives for action based on choice.

Story Time

Subject Area: Reading
Grade Level: 3–8
Time: Ongoing

Objectives

1. Students will become interested in reading highly acclaimed books that represent diverse peoples in both text and illustrations.

2. Students will enjoy a variety of books both above and below their instructional levels.

3. Students will learn that some groups of people are oppressed and that oppression can manifest itself in many forms.

4. Students will analyze and synthesize ideas in stories.

5. Students will understand that reading is a prerequisite to the acquisition of certain types of knowledge, as well as a necessity for taking advantage of certain types of opportunities.

6. Students will generate alternatives to social conditions that restrict opportunities for oppressed groups of people and develop strategies for their accomplishment.

Suggested Procedures

1. Select trade books, especially those dealing with issues pertaining to race, class, gender, or disability, to read to students throughout the school year, such as the following: *Baseball Saved Us,* by K. Mochizuki; *Family Pictures/Cuadros de Familia,* by Carmen Lomas Garza; *Felita* and its sequel, *Going Home,* by Nicholasa Mohr; *The Hot and Cold Summer,* by J. Hurwitz; *Hundred Penny Box,* by Sharon Bell Mathis; *My Friend Jacob,* by L. Clifton; *Silent Lotus,* by Jeanne M. Lee; *Slake's Limbo,* by Felice Holman; *Smoky Night,* by E. Bunting; *Tar Beach,* by F. Ringgold ; and *The Well,* by M. D. Taylor.

2. Develop a set of discussion questions related to the issues presented in the book. If the book is lengthy and will span two or three weeks, develop a series of questions to follow sections of the book. Alternatively—and in order to generate more student-centered learning—you may want to incorporate into this lesson teaching students how to write good discussion questions (e.g., using the question-answer relationship (QAR) typology developed by (Raphael, 1982, 1986). The QAR includes four types of questions—"Right There Questions," "Search and Find Questions," "Author and You Questions," and "On My Own Questions." When I use the QAR with students, I have printed material or a power point to demonstrate each of the questions. Raphael (1982, 1986) explains that Right There Questions, or literal questions, are ones where the correct answer is probably somewhere in the passage the students just read. This is usually an easy one for students to understand. The Search and Find Questions require a bit more effort because students have to relate ideas or information in the material to each other. Here I actively work with the students because when they get this idea, I say, "We are halfway home and this will help you for life." Here I help students to look back at the passage to find the information that the question refers to, and

(Continued)

then have them think about how the information or ideas fit together. Author and You Questions ask students to use ideas and information that are not stated directly in the passage to answer the questions. The examples Raphael (1982, 1986) gives are: "The author implies . . . ," "The passage. Suggests . . . ," "The speaker's attitude. . . ." With the Author and You Questions, I tell students to make careful, informed leaps; they do it all the time when they are trying to scope out what's going on with their friends: What data are you putting together to determine who likes whom? On My Own Questions are answered using the students' own background knowledge, according to Raphael (1982, 1986). Examples of these include "In your opinion. . . ." and "Based on your experience. . . ." Here, I have students take something from What they read and relate it to their own life circumstances. After teaching students about QAR, the students' responsibility will be to write at least one of the four kinds of questions about their reading, with the intention of crafting questions that require higher-order thinking (e.g., synthesis and analysis). By teaching students to take control of the discussions of these books, they are able to engage in a more authentic, shared inquiry process.

3. As time permits, read a book (or a portion of a book) to students each day. Following the reading, have the class discuss issues raised in the reading, guided by the teacher's planned questions. This can be done in small groups or with the whole class. Alternatively, and in order to draw on multiple intelligences in your classroom rather than another discussion, you might engage in a more multimodal, cooperative activity such as a "Chart Talk." In a Chart Talk, students are split into small groups. Each student receives a different-colored marker and a sheet of chart paper with a question, quote, or drawing related to the reading. Without speaking, students engage in a "silent" conversation in their Chart Talk, writing and drawing in response to the initial prompt as well as one another's comments and questions. Focus specifically on issues related to race, class, gender, or disability in the story, probing for their relationship to story events. For example, probe the causes that led the boys in *The Hot and Cold Summer* to have preconceived stereotypic ideas about what the girl who was coming to visit would be like. It is often necessary to role-play parts of the story to give students a feeling for events from the viewpoint of the characters, especially when using stories outside children's experiential background, such as having a disability or living in an urban area when they do not. A fun way to encourage role-playing is the "Hot Seat" a small group of students each takes on the identity of one of the characters from the story, and the rest of the class is able to "interview" the characters about the events of the story as well as about more hypothetical and inferential aspects of the character. Students are interviewed "in character" and respond to their classmates'

questions as if they were the character in the book. Students can take turns with the same character, or you can have a panel of multiple characters at once. This is an effective way of digging into themes and inferences that is not dependent on students' reading level. It may be helpful for the teacher to keep a journal of students' reactions to the books and to the discussions generated in class, as well as of ongoing evidence of improvement in their reading ability. The journal will help the teacher to see visible evidence of change in the students as individuals, in the class as a whole, and in the teacher's own practice.

4. Encourage students to generate alternative courses of action for the story characters based on earlier discussions of story events and to consider all applicable consequences to these alternatives. The teacher may want to ask for volunteers to state the alternative they prefer and to explain their rationale. Discussion follows as other volunteers agree and disagree and offer alternative rationales. The teacher will be able to assess the extent to which students are critically analyzing and synthesizing issues related to race, class, gender, and disability. The teacher needs to provide a nonthreatening environment for doing this. Since much of what one believes comes from one's experiential background, the teacher must be aware of students' ability to understand the issues and should guide the discussion so that students experience a wide variety of ideas and rationales. The teacher also should help students to analyze their own backgrounds for experiences with oppression, either as oppressors or as the oppressed, which is best done in a nonthreatening way using examples from the story.

5. On completion of a book, give students a choice of projects related to the story. The class, either as a whole or in small groups, should decide in a democratic fashion on a follow-up activity that they believe is suitable for that particular book. The teacher should provide a short list of alternative projects and explore with the class the pros and cons of each one. The list of activities may vary but should end with one that allows students to design their own projects. The following are some examples that could be used:

    a. After reading *The Hot and Cold Summer*, students will have discussed the origins of sex role stereotypes and how those stereotypes are broken down, and they will have speculated about the ability of the boys in the story to apply what they have learned about one female to all females. A small group of students then interviews younger students about their nontraditional roles (e.g., boys who enjoy playing with dolls or girls who enjoy playing with cars and trucks). The older students work with their younger partners to create a language experience book about that child. The finished product may be bound or laminated and

(Continued)

(Continued)

shared with the younger student's peers. The younger child reads the book to a small group of classmates, and the older child leads a discussion of nontraditional roles in an effort to break down stereotypes held by those children and to reinforce issues of equity. This activity not only gives older students an opportunity to become actively involved in promoting change, but it can open the door for ongoing cooperative partnerships between older and younger students as well.

b. A small group of students reads another book dealing with the same or a related issue as the book discussed in class and then prepares a comparison between the two books. They may choose to read the book to the class and lead a discussion, or they may meet with the teacher to discuss their analysis. For example, following *The Hot and Cold Summer,* the class could read *Amazing Grace* by Mary Hoffman and discuss preconceived notions of ethnicity as it relates to theatrical role assignments. Since both books deal with strong, positive, female protagonists, the theme can become explicit as the teacher addresses gender and ethnic stereotypes.

c. In small groups, students rewrite the story (or part of the story) in play form, incorporating one or more of the alternatives and its consequences as discussed in class. As students rewrite the story, they should role-play the scenes to get a feel for the dialogue and the feasibility of the chosen alternative. The finished play can be produced with costumes and scenery and performed for the rest of the class.

d. The class can research the author(s) of texts read in class. They can then compile a list of issue-related questions that they would like to ask the author. The list can be sent to the author or publisher with a cover letter written by the group that explains its discussion of the issue and its interest in the book. If feasible, the group could invite the author to the school. When a high school class in California did this, the popular author Terry McMillan came to the school for a visit! She discussed her ideas and rationale for character development, plot, and the image of African American women that her works portray.

Two or three students can prepare the story and a plan for discussion with the students in the role of book leader. The story is then read and discussed in another class with the students as readers and discussion leaders.

Students rewrite the story (or part of it) from another person's perspective (e.g., having a disability versus not having a disability), with a different ending (perhaps more realistic), with a different protagonist (e.g., Latino instead of European

American), or in a different setting (e.g., suburban rather than inner city).

e. Older students rewrite difficult or longer stories for younger students. Pages may be illustrated, laminated, and bound. The books are read to and discussed with younger children by older children. Also, older students may write their own personal version of the story, using events and experiences from their own lives related to the selected theme.

f. The teacher should maintain a reading center in the class so that the students have available to them a wide variety of books that address the themes being discussed in class. Once they understand the format, students should be encouraged to develop their own literature circles whenever possible.

6. If the projects are done in small groups rather than as a class, students should meet as a whole class and share their projects. They should tell their classmates what they did, explain how and why they chose their projects, and detail their analysis of the results.

Evaluation

1. Assess students' enthusiasm for the books being read to them through their attentiveness and their own selection of books at later dates.

2. Assess students' levels of discussion following the readings.

3. Assess the quality of students' project activities and the sharing of projects.

4. Determine the extent of students' carryover discussion of issues related to oppressed groups and social inequality into other content areas.

5. Assess students' improvement in reading ability as evidenced in all subject areas.

Example I References

Bell Mathis, S. (1975). *The hundred penny box.* New York: Viking Press.
Bunting, E. (1994). *Smoky night.* San Diego: Harcourt Brace.
Clifton, L. (1980). *My friend Jacob.* New York: E. P. Dutton.
Curtis, C. (1998). *The Watsons go to Birmingham-1963.* Bel Air CA: Yearling.
Curtis, C. (1999). *Bud not buddy.* New York: Delacorte.
Garza, C. L. (1990). *Family pictures/Cuadros de familia.* San Francisco: Children's Book Press.

Hoffman, M. (1998). *Amazing grace*. New York: Penguin Books.

Holman, F. (1977). *Slakes limbo*. New York: Scribner.

Hurwitz, J. (1985). *The hot and cold summer*. New York: Scholastic.

Kadohata, C. (2004). *Kira-Kira*. New York: Atheneum.

Lee, J. M. (1991). *Silent lotus*. New York: Farrar, Straus & Giroux.

Mochizuki, K. (1993). *Baseball saved us*. New York: Lee & Low Books.

Mohr, N. (1996). *Felita*. New York: Penguin Books.

Mohr, N. (1999). *Going home*. New York: Penguin Books.

Park, L. S. (2001). *A single shard*. New York: Clarion.

Ringgold, F. (1991). *Tar beach*. New York: Crown.

Taylor, M. D. (1976). *Roll of thunder, hear my cry*. New York: Dial.

Taylor, M. D. (1995). *The well*. New York: Dial Books for Young Readers.

EXAMPLE II

Bring together your colleagues who teach at the primary level and share with them that you plan to take action in dealing with the achievement gaps and diversity. Next, explain to them how you are implementing change. Share with them this family unit that addresses diverse family structures and focuses on language arts and English language development. Tell them that each activity has been modified with the sensitivity that marginalized groups are not usually introduced into the classroom curriculum. Point out that the teacher who developed the plan asked students about what a family is; students answered with the "traditional family portrait": mom, dad, brothers, and sisters. When asked if they knew of other family types, only those experiencing the nontraditional family responded with examples of a single parent or being raised by grandparents.

Be aware that some of your teacher/friends may not feel that kindergartners are capable of this type of lesson that includes gay and lesbian parents. The teacher who created the unit soon overcame this underestimation of the students' ability to learn. At the time of planning this unit, she pondered the ability of her students to be able to discuss and gain knowledge from this learning experience. As it turned out, their oral histories were very explicit and colorful to listen to. She used her own life experiences, especially being an educator of color. Her experiences often paralleled the children's lives, which made this learning experience even more enjoyable. Using the book *Family Pictures*, she would remind the students that she herself went through many of those experiences. Personalizing this book made the students want to draw more information from their teacher, who reminded them (but most of all herself) that her heritage and culture was very important.

This grade level should not be held back for fear of not being able to make this learning experience worthwhile. Educators must project their own enthusiasm to the learning experience, "grab them" with whatever it takes, and don't let go. This lesson, as with any, would not have been attempted with any risk of a negative learning outcome.

Families

Subject Area: Multiple areas
Grade Level: K–2
Time: One week
Students: English language learners (ELL)

Objectives

1. Students will describe and identify the members of their own families and answer questions about their family using the high-frequency word "*mí.*"
2. Students will identify the makeup of a traditional family, a single-parent family, a gay- or lesbian-headed family, a grandparent-headed family, an extended family, and multiple generations living together in a single home.
3. Students will distinguish between an activity performed indoors and one performed outdoors.
4. Students will use symbolic and D'Nealian-style writing.
5. Students will compare and contrast nontraditional families using key English vocabulary including mother, father, son, daughter, sister, brother, stepmother, stepfather, and so on.

Suggested Procedures

1. To introduce the week's theme, have the class brainstorm questions on what a family looks like and acts like. (The teacher may wish to prod students to define family as more than the people that make it up; for example, a family is a group of people who love and care for each other.)

2. Have the class as a whole use magazine cutouts to create a collage that shows families from various countries, cultures, and types. The teacher contributes to the collage by including every family type on which the week focuses. Follow this activity with a whole-class discussion that brings out the idea that families are made up of many different people. Encourage the children to introduce their own families. Tell them that they will learn about their classroom members' families more in depth.

3. Show and read *Antonio's Card/La Tarjeta de Antonio*, where a young boy learns that love defines a family, no matter what it looks like. For older students, you could also use the novel *The Music of Dolphins* by Karen Hesse, in which dominant society is forced to transform their ideas about family and parenting.

(Continued)

(Continued)

4. Show the children the illustrations on the cover and title page of the book *Con Mi Familia* (written by Olga Ramero, illustrated by Pauline Rodriquez Howard). In this story, a little girl introduces her family and what they do together. Read the title; then tell the children that they will get to know the family in the story. As they look at the title page, ask them to make predictions about the story. Read the story as you point under each word to help children connect speech to print.

5. Have the children construct family portraits as an art project. Have them decide who will be included in their family portrait (nuclear, extended, blended), and how many adults and children that is. Help children label family members with their names. Ask children to describe their completed pictures with family member names, their relationship, and any other information they wish to give. To practice the high-frequency word *mí*, ask students to tell their teacher, "*mí* . . . es . . . " responding to the familial pictures they drew.

6. The next day, read *La Cama de Mamá/Mama's Bed* (written by Joi Carlen, illustrated by Morella Fuenmayor). This is a story about a family of three and what they can do in their mother's bed, such as playing, being held, and sleeping. As a writing activity, have students copy today's date onto the first line on the top right-hand side of the paper. Ask them, "What do you and your family members do at bedtime?" Model appropriate conventions of writing and letter formation. Students then write symbolic and D'Nealian-style responses. Students draw a picture to match their written response.

7. On the third day of the unit, read and discuss *One Dad, Two Dads, Brown Dad, Blue Dads* (written by Johnny Valentine, illustrated by Melody Sarecky). In this book, a girl questions a boy about his two blue-skinned dads, who are gay. She discovers that despite their blueness, they do all the usual things that other dads do. Follow up by having students draw pictures of their families in their favorite family activity. Then have students sort the activities and place them according to indoor or outdoor activities on the classroom chart.

8. The next day, read and discuss *Heather Has Two Mommies* (written by Leslea Newman, illustrated by Diana Souza). This is a story about Heather, whose favorite number is two. She has two arms, two legs, and so on; she also has two mommies. Have available a basket of books about different family structures. During drop everything and read (DEAR) time, have students choose books from this basket. For English language development, ask students, using English, to recall and identify the different family members as the books are individually displayed. Have them describe different family structures by choosing

people and displaying them on the felt board to represent each book. A second book for this activity is *Mom and Mum Are Getting Married*, by Ken Setterington. It is about love and happiness in a changing world.

9. For the last day of the unit, create a big book of families, using students' art and writing projects. Title it *Con Mi Familia* (our version). Invite families to join the class, participating in various activities throughout their school day. Share this book with the class and their families.

Evaluation

1. Evaluate students' understanding and appreciation of family members, family relationships, and multiple family structures based on their writings and class discussion.

2. Evaluate students' use of D'Nealian-style writing based on their writing samples; identify letters they are having difficulty making for further instruction and practice.

3. Evaluate students' ability to use high-frequency words in both English and Spanish through their oral discussion of their families.

4. Identify students' comprehension of indoors and outdoors based on sorting activity.

SOURCE: From *Turning On Learning: Five Approach to Multicultural Teaching Plans for Race, Class, Gender and Disability* (5th ed), by Carl A. Grant and Christine E. Sleeter. Copyright Wiley, 2008. Reprinted with permission of John Wiley & Sons, Inc.

Example II References

Carlen, J., & Fuenmayor, M. (Illustrator). (2000). *La cama de Mamá/Mama's bed.* Volcano, CA: Volcano Press.

Gonzales, R. (2005). *Antonio's card/La tarjeta de Antonio.* Illustrated by Cecilia Conceapcion Alvarez. San Francisco: Children's Book Press.

Newman, L., & Souza, D. (Illustrator). (2000). *Heather has two mommies.* Boston: Alyson.

Romero, O., & Rodriguez Howard, P. (1998). *Con mi familia.* Carmel, CA: Hampton-Brown.

Setterington, K., & Priestly, A. (Illustrator). (2004). *Mom and mum are getting married.* Toronto, Ontario, Canada: Second Story Press.

Valentine, J., & Sarecky, M. (Illustrator). (1994). *One dad, two dads, brown dad, blue dads.* Boston: Alyson.

EXAMPLE III

Bring together your colleagues who teach at the middle or high school level and share with them that you plan to take action in dealing with the achievement gaps and diversity. Next, explain to them how you are implementing change.

Begin by saying that you are going to start with the lesson, "Local Government," which is designed to capture the interest and concerns of young adolescents, especially the ones who live in the city and enjoy issue-oriented activities in which they can express values that are important to them. Remind your teacher/friends that the research and best practice literature argues that students internalize concepts more readily that apply to their daily lives.

This plan has students examine what diverse groups compose a city, town, and/or rural area and then analyze competing claims that different groups have on local service resources. It includes activities in which students role-play a local council and have to collectively decide how to allocate resources. By examining the allocation of resources of a city, town, or rural area and by role-playing a local government council, students will learn that resources are often distributed unequally and that the decision-making process can produce that result. In addition, by collecting and discussing newspaper articles on local services in their own city, town, or rural area, students can begin to apply this analysis to where they live.

Local Government

Subject Area: Social Studies
Grade Level: 7–10
Time: One or two weeks

Objectives

1. Students will describe an urban, local, or rural area in terms of a variety of ethnic, racial, age, and religious groups, each with its own needs.

2. Students will demonstrate sensitivity to these diverse needs.

3. Students will identify necessary local services.

4. Students will recognize that areas should make local services equally available to a diverse population.

5. Students will view decision making as a necessary part of running a local community.

6. Students will learn that mutual cooperation is one method of solving common local government problems.

7. Students will recognize that local services have an impact on the quality of urban life.

8. Students will appreciate that cultural diversity makes a local area a "better place."

Suggested Procedures

1. Do a walking field trip with students so that they can record data on persons they see out and about in the area. Have the students present the data they collected to the class and record their responses for the class to see.

2. As a class, discuss how the needs of a diverse population vary from group to group (e.g., neighborhoods with large numbers of children need more schools; limited-English-speaking communities need services in their own languages; a neighborhood center could serve the young after school and the elderly during the day).

3. As a group, students should determine what local services could meet these diverse needs.

4. Present the following scenario to the class: "You are all members of a local government council. It is your job to determine which local services will be funded in the neighborhood described in the accompanying packet. You may not go over budget and you will have to make decisions. There is not enough money for everything this area needs. As a group, you should give attention to how you solve this problem (through bullying, coopera-tion, and so on) as well as to solving the problem itself. Be prepared to describe to the class how you resolved this issue and what you actually decided." As an additional civics lesson, such as in Schultz's (2008) class-room, students can engage in inquiry-based research on different aspects of the local government: funding processes, structure of the government, cur-rent events, and issues in their local area, and so forth. Before beginning the aforementioned role-playing activity, students could do this research in order to inform their role-playing and to more accurately consider how the local government runs. Such research might open doors to critiques of how the local government currently runs and might lead to further research comparing local government structures, looking at how a single issue is dealt with across multiple cities, locating the "origins" of democracy, and tracing what different, modern forms of democracy look like.

5. Give each group a packet that includes the following items (this could be structured so that either the teacher presents this information or students gather it):
   a. Map of the area
   b. List of needs for the area
   c. Population (who lives there?)
   d. Possible local services that could meet needs (Each local ser-vice should be given a fixed dollar amount that it would cost to implement.)
   e. Amount of money the council has to spend (must be less than what is needed for all services, so decisions have to be made)

(Continued)

(Continued)

6. In small groups, students should discuss and decide which local government services they feel should be implemented in "their neighborhood." Remind them that they should decide how they want to make these decisions and present their findings. Their presentations should include the local government services that should be implemented in the area, an explanation of how each service will meet the needs of the area, reasons the service was chosen over other services, and the way the group arrived at its decision (i.e., the group decision-making process).

7. Once all group projects have been presented, the teacher should guide the class in drawing some conclusions. Discuss the following questions and ideas:

   a. How does availability of local government services affect the quality of your lives? For example, how good would your education be if it was in a language you did not understand? Is a new bus line good for you if the bus stops six or seven blocks from your house or it is impossible for you to get on?

   b. How does availability of local government services affect the quality of city life as a whole (e.g., health clinics that reduce the spread of communicable diseases)?

   c. How do the local government services available to you make your lives better in the long term versus the short term? For example, if the school is two blocks from your house, how does its close proximity affect your feelings about it?

   d. Local governments always have to make some kind of decision about which service to supply and how it will be implemented in a city. This has the potential to be a heated, emotional decision in real life, and students need to discuss the kinds of behaviors that help ensure a fair decision-making process. They should refer back to their own discussions and identify behaviors that allowed for an open discussion (also discuss why an open discussion is in the best interest of all people).

8. Have students collect newspaper articles about current local government service issues. They should present in written or oral form what they consider the issue to be and how it relates to quality of life within their city, town, or rural area. Alternatively, have students write persuasive letters to the editor of the newspaper(s) about the issues they researched and to argue their opinions and perspective. In addition, students could convene a town hall meeting at the school to which they invite parents, community members, and their city councilperson.

Evaluation

1. Assess students' appreciation of the diversity of an urban population through initial class discussion and their participation in the mock local government council.

2. Assess students' understanding of local government services through their solutions to the groups' problems.

3. Assess students' decision-making skills through their small-group work, particularly after having taught students how to make cooperative decisions (see Kagan, 1985).

SOURCE: From *Turning On Learning: Five Approach to Multicultural Teaching Plans for Race, Class, Gender and Disability* (5th ed.), by Carl A. Grant and Christine E. Sleeter. Copyright Wiley, 2008. Reprinted with permission of John Wiley & Sons, Inc.

EXAMPLE IV

Bring together your colleagues who teach at the middle school level and share with them that you plan to take action in dealing with the achievement gap and diversity. More specifically, you are going to teach your students how to make/write a persuasive argument by using a topic that will capture the interest of most middle school students. Next explain that you will teach the lesson, "Advertising for an Audience." The lesson is a critical analysis of advertising and will help students develop a greater understanding about consumerism and how power works. Remind your teacher/friends that although media literacy is becoming more common in schools, it is still not a part of the curriculum in most U.S. schools; however, people are bombarded with media messages daily. Many of these messages, and particularly advertising, are carefully designed to get people to act in a particular way, with most advertising trying to get people to spend money on a certain product.

Explain that the lesson teaches students not only to identify product market audiences and techniques used to persuade those audiences but also how buying power is connected to what we see in the media. In other words, messages in the mass media are designed to appeal to segments of the public that have money. Also note that the plan encourages students to pay attention to different audiences (e.g., young, old, affluent) where products are marketed. In addition, companies who buy the advertisements make the decision about the content of the messages as well as about the people who deliver the message. Further explain that the plan extends this analysis to examine who benefits from the profits the companies make. In other words, it gets students to ask, "Where does the money go?" "What kinds of employment and social relations is it supporting?" Students will learn that companies vary widely; some are quite socially responsible, while others are not.

Advertising for an Audience

Subject Area: Language Arts
Grade Level: 6–12
Time: Four class periods

Objectives

1. Students will identify the audience to whom an advertisement was directed and what that advertisement wants the audience to do.

2. Students will identify techniques the advertiser used to appeal to that audience.

3. Students will identify who profits by their spending money in response to the advertisement.

4. Students will create a message for that audience, raising their awareness about advertising and its connection to money.

5. Students will observe the race, gender, and social class demographics of the people used in the advertisement.

6. Students will observe that people from some groups are often not included in certain advertisements or, when included, are shown in a minor role.

Suggested Procedures

1. Instruct students to each bring an advertisement to class. It can be from a magazine, a newspaper, the Internet, or a description of an ad on TV.

2. Briefly discuss how easy it was to locate advertisements and the degree to which advertisements permeate our surroundings. Make sure that everyone can distinguish commercial advertisements from the program or story itself, since young people sometimes may not see these as different. Discuss ways in which advertising blends with magazine stories or TV shows, such as products featured in TV shows, movies, or infomercials.

3. Select four to six advertisements students brought and divide the class into groups. Each group should take one advertisement. Have them answer the following questions:

- What demographic group is the ad targeted to? Look at the race/ethnicity, age, gender, and socioeconomic status of the people featured in the ad and the magazine, TV show, or other source in which the ad was placed.

- What does the advertisement want to get the audience to do?

- What techniques does it use to do this? For example, does the ad use someone the target audience might identify with? Does it try to make the target audience feel deficient without the advertised product?

This analysis could be connected with types of appeals and named persuasive techniques (e.g., red herrings); after engaging in this analysis, students could learn some of the formal categories of persuasive techniques and appeals and then sort their self-determined techniques into these more formal categories. By connecting this lesson on advertisements to persuasive techniques, not only can you foster a social justice curriculum, but you can also hit on frequently tested material.

4. Discuss each group's analysis. Students should see that advertisements generally try to get people to spend money and are targeted at specific audiences. Some demographic groups are rarely targeted at all; others are targeted repeatedly. Help students to identify which groups are commonly targeted by advertisers and for which kinds of products. For example, students might identify ads for alcohol as common in Black and Latino neighborhoods; ads for cleaning products as commonly targeted at women; many ads targeted at young, white, upwardly mobile people; and few targeted at people who are poor.

5. Have students examine the advertisements in *Ebony* and *Latina* and on television channels that carry Black and Latino programming. Have students compare them with the advertisements in the mainstream media discussed above.

6. Have students analyze what proportion of a medium (such as TV, magazines) consists of advertising. For example, how many minutes of a half-hour TV show or how many pages of a magazine consist of advertisements? Investigate ways in which advertisers influence the content of media. Some helpful sources on the Internet are listed below:

Fairness and Accuracy in Reporting (FAIR) www.fair.org

Global Issues That Affect Everyone www.globalissues.org

National Labor Committee www.nlcnet.org

Public Citizen, Ralph Nader's consumer rights/social justice organization www.citizen.org

7. Select a company that advertises extensively to young people. Have students find out as much as they can about the following items:

- Who owns the company
- Racial and gender composition of their board of directors

(Continued)

(Continued)

- What kind of affirmative action hiring and promotion policy they have
- Their environmental record
- Their fair labor policies
- Political and community organizations they contribute to

8. Have a discussion about where students' money goes when they purchase products, and who benefits most from that flow of money (and influence).

9. Have students design and produce an advertisement that raises awareness about advertising, money flow, and corporate profit, and target that advertisement to an audience of their peers.

Evaluation

1. Evaluate the extent to which students are able to identify audiences and the techniques advertisers use to appeal to audiences. Use small group reports and class discussion.

2. Evaluate the extent to which students are able to connect advertising with corporate profit through their discussion of research into companies.

3. Evaluate the extent to which students are able to use these techniques themselves to speak to a specific audience through the awareness-raising advertisement they develop.

SOURCE: From *Turning On Learning: Five Approach to Multicultural Teaching Plans for Race, Class, Gender and Disability* (5th ed.), by Carl A. Grant and Christine E. Sleeter. Copyright Wiley, 2008. Reprinted with permission of John Wiley & Sons, Inc.

Example 3 Resources

Graydon, S. (2003). *Made you look: How advertising works and why you should know.* Toronto, Ontario, Canada: Anmick Press.
Nye, N. S. (2005). *Going, going.* New York: Greenwillow: Harper.

Conclusion

You must be the change you wish to see in the world.

—Gandhi

Ten chapters ago, you and several of your teacher/friends came together to contribute to a solution for eliminating the achievement gaps and making schooling more academically gratifying and culturally relevant for your students. In doing so, you participated in an exciting and, at times, challenging learning experience as you and your teacher/friends engaged in the change/transition process. The expectations for and challenges of closing the achievement gap and affirming diversity are great. Both will require your constant vigilance and this requirement, in essence, means that this work—your work—is not done. Thankfully—and I hope you see it that way—neither is your giving to and receiving support from your teacher/friends over. Hopefully, what you and your teacher/friends have learned from working together to complete these activities and meet the challenges of change/transition and affirming diversity is that it is a lot more fun and rewarding when you work with others. Together, you have learned how to speak "truth to power" and how to push back, professionally and intelligently, and with the best interests of both students and our democratic society in mind, against the current trends of reforms that call for an apolitical schooling that reduces learning to rote memorization and teaching to scripted curriculum.

I loudly and vigorously applaud your work. I know it was not easy, and at times you probably asked, "Is it worth it?" Now, how do you answer the question, "Is it worth it?" Without too much hesitation, I believe that your answer is, "Yes!" Each of you—if I may take a bit of liberty with Gandhi's statement—must become and are becoming the change you wish to see in the world. You are realizing that the change will not happen unless you actively participate. Theodore Roosevelt stated that "victory belongs to those who enter the arena." To bring about change/ transition, to provide a solution to the achievement gap, and to affirm diversity, not only must teachers enter the arena, but they must work hard to invest in solutions for tomorrow.

References

Álvarez, A. N., & Miville, M. L. (2003). Walking a tightrope: Strategies for teaching under-graduate multicultural counseling courses. In D. Pope-Davis, W. Liu, & R. Toporek (Eds.), *Handbook of multicultural competencies in counseling and psychology* (pp. 528–547). Thousand Oaks, CA: Sage.

American Council of Education. (1995). *Educating America for a world in flux.* Washington, DC: American Council of Education.

Andrade, A. M., & Hakim, D. (1995). Letting children take the lead in class. *Educational Leadership, 53*(1), 22–24.

Bandura, A., Barbaranelli, C., Caprara, G. V., & Pastorelli, C. (1996). Multifaceted impact of self-efficacy beliefs on academic functioning. *Child Development, 67*, 1206–1222.

Bandura, A., Barbaranelli, C., Vittorio, C., & Pastorelli, C. (2001). Self-efficacy beliefs as shapers of children's aspirations and career trajectories. *Child Development, 72*(1), 1987–2006.

Barr, A. S. (1950). Teaching competencies. In W. S. Monroe (Ed.), *Encyclopedia of educational research* (pp. 1446–1454). New York: Macmillan.

Beaudin, L., & Hadden, C. (2004). Developing technopedagogical skills in pre-service teachers. In G. Richards (Ed.), *Proceedings of World Conference on E-Learning in Corporate, Government, Healthcare, and Higher Education 2004* (pp. 492–498). Chesapeake, VA: American Association College Education.

Bergson, H. (n.d.). *Famous Henri Bergson quotes.* Retrieved April 22, 2009, from http://en .thinkexist.com/quotes/henri_bergson

Blanchett, J. (2006). Disproportionate representation of African American students in special education: Acknowledging the role of white privilege and racism. *Educational Researcher, 35*(6), 24–28.

Boger, J. C., & Orfield, G. (2005). *School resegregation: Must the South turn back?* Chapel Hill: University of North Carolina Press.

Bridges, W. (2003). *Managing transitions: Making the most of change* (2nd ed.). New York: Perseus Books.

Carter, P. (2005). *Keepin' it real: School success beyond black and white.* New York: Oxford University Press.

Chin, R., & Benne, K. (1976). General strategies for effecting changes in human systems. In W. Bennis, K. Benne, R. Chin, & K. Corey (Eds.), *The planning of change* (3rd ed., pp. 22–45). New York: Holt, Rinehart, & Winston.

Cohen, E., & Lotan, R. (1997). *Working for equity in heterogeneous classrooms: Sociological theory in action.* New York: Teachers College Press.

Collopy, R., & Green, T. (1995). Using motivational theory with at-risk children. *Educational Leadership, 53*(1), 41–43.

Connelly, M., Clandinin J. D., & He, M. F. (1997). Teachers' personal practical knowledge on the professional knowledge landscape. *Teaching and Teacher Education, 13*(7), 665–674.

Cooper, C. W. (2003). The detrimental impact of teacher bias: Lessons learned from the standpoint of African American mother. *Teacher Education Quarterly, 30*(2), 101–116.

Cornbleth, C. (2008). *Diversity and the new teacher: Learning from experience in urban schools.* New York: Teachers College Press,

Delpit, L. (1996). *Other people's children: Cultural conflict in the classroom.* New York: New Press.

Dewey, J. (1977). The child and the curriculum. In A. Bellack, & H. Kliebard (Eds.), *Curriculum and evaluation* (pp. 175–188). Berkeley, CA: McCutchan.

Dilworth, M., & Brown, A. (2008). Teachers of color: Quality and effective teachers one way or another. In M. Cochran-Smith, S. Feiman-Nemser, D. J. McIntyre, & K. Demers (Eds.), *Handbook of research on teacher education: Enduring question in changing contexts* (3rd ed., pp. 424–444). New York: Routledge.

Dodd, A. (1995). Engaging students: What I learned along the way. *Educational Leadership, 53*(1), 65–69.

Du Bois, W. E. B. (1994). *The souls of Black folk.* Avenel, NJ: Gramercy Books.

Eck, D. (1997). *A new religious America: How a "Christian country" has become the world's most religiously diverse nation.* San Francisco: Harper.

Farkas, G. (2004). The black-white test score gap. *Contexts, 3*(2), 12–21.

Finn, C., Jr. (2008, Spring). Troublemaker: The education of Chester Finn. *Education Next, 8*(2), 22–29.

Foucault, M. (1977). *Discipline and punish: The birth of the prison* (A. Sheridan, Trans.). New York: Random House.

Freire, P. (1970). *Pedagogy of the oppressed.* New York: Continuum.

Friedman, T. L. (2006). *The world is flat.* New York: Farrar, Straus & Giroux.

Friedman, T. L. (2008). *Hot, flat and crowded.* New York: Farrar, Straus & Giroux.

Fultz, M. (1995). African American teachers in the south, 1890–1940: Powerlessness and the ironies of expectations and protest. *History of Education Quarterly, 35*(4), 401–422.

Gardner, H. (1993). *Frames of mind: The theory of multiple intelligence.* New York: Basic Books.

Gay, G. (1975). Organizing and designing culturally pluralistic curriculum. *Educational Leadership, 33,* 176–183.

Gay, G. (1993). Building cultural bridges: A bold proposal for teacher education. *Education and Urban Society, 25*(3), 285–299.

Grant, C. A. (1977). The mediator of culture: A teacher role revisited. *Journal of Research and Development in Education, 11*(1), 102–117.

Grant, C. A., & Sleeter, C. F. (2007). *Making choices for multicultural education.* New York: John Wiley & Son.

Grossman, P., McDonald, M., Hammerness, K., & Ronfeldt, M. (2008). Dismantling dichotomies in teacher education. In M. Cochran-Smith, S. Feiman-Nemser, D. J. McIntyre, & K. Demers (Eds.), *Handbook of research on teacher education: Enduring question in changing contexts* (3rd ed., pp. 243–248). New York: Routledge.

Haberman, M. (1995). *Star teachers of children of poverty.* Bloomington, IN: Kappa Delta Pi.

Hanushek, E. A., Lavy. V., & Kohtaru, H. (2008). Do students care about school quality? Determinants of dropout behavior in developing countries. *Journal of Human Capital, 2*(1). Retrieved June 7, 2008, from http://www.journals.uchicago.edu/doi/abs/10.1086/529446

Howitt, D., & Owusu-Bempah, J. (1990). Racism in a British journal? *Psychologist,* (3), 396–400.

Irvine, J. I. (2001). *Caring, competent teachers in complex classrooms* (41st Charles W. Hunt Memorial Lecture). Washington, DC: American Association of Colleges for Teacher Education.

Jacobsen, J., Olsen, C., Rice, J. K., Sweetland, S., & Ralph, J. (2004). *Educational achievement and black-white inequality.* Washington, DC: National Center for Education Statistics.

Jencks, C., & Phillips, M (1998). *The black-white test score gap.* Washington, DC: Brooking Institution Press.

Jersild, A. (1955). *When teachers face themselves.* New York: Teachers College Press.

Kagan, S. (1985). *Cooperative learning.* San Clemente, CA: Kagan.

Kinney, L. B. (1953). *Measure of a good teacher.* San Francisco: California Teachers Association.

Killen, M., McGlothlin, H., & Henning, A. (2007). Explicit judgment and implicit attitudes: A developmental perspective. In S. R. Levy & M. Killen (Eds.), *Intergroup relations: An integrative developmental and social psychological perspective* (pp. 126–145). Oxford, UK: Oxford University Press.

King, J. (1991). Dysconscious racism: Identity, ideology, and the miseducation of teachers. *Journal of Negro Education, 60*(2), 133–146.

Kossek, E. E., & Zonia, S. (1993). Assessing diversity climate: A field study of reactions to employer efforts to promote diversity. *Journal of Organizational Behavior, 14,* 16–81.

Kumar, S. (2007). *Creating conducive classroom climate.* Retrieved November 20, 2008, from www.articlesbase.com/education-articles/creating-conducive-classroom-climate-256406.html—53ki

Ladson-Billings, G. (1994). *The dreamkeepers: Successful teachers of African-American children.* San Francisco: Jossey-Bass.

Ladson-Billings, G. J. (1995). Toward a theory of culturally relevant pedagogy. *American Education Research Journal, 35,* 465–491.

Lee, E. Menkart, D., & Okazawa-Rey, M. (1998). *Beyond heroes and holidays: A practical guide to K–12 antiracist, multicultural education and staff development.* Washington, DC: Network of Educators on the Americas.

Liu, W. M., & Pope-Davis, D. B. (2003). Moving from diversity to multiculturalism: Exploring power and its implications for multicultural competence. In D. B. Pope-Davis, H. L. K. Coleman, W. M. Liu, & R. L. Toporek (Eds.), *Handbook of multicultural competencies in counseling & psychology* (pp. 90–102). Thousand Oaks, CA: Sage.

McCall, M. S., Hauser, C., Cronin, J., Kingsbury, G. G., Houser, R. (2006). *Achievement gaps: An examination of differences in student achievement and growth.* Lake Oswego, OR: Northwest Evaluation Association.

Musselwhite, C., & Jones, R. (2004). *Dangerous opportunity: Making change work.* Bloomington, IN: Xlibris Corporation.

National Education Association. (1997). *Study of the American public school teacher, 1995–96.* Washington, DC: National Education Association.

National Education Association. (2004). *NEA Foundation Initiative: Closing the achievement gaps.* Washington, DC. National Education Association.

The National Governors Association. (2007). Center for Best Practices. Retrieved April 10, 2008, from http://www.google.com/search?q=cache:I121ubLlDQJ:www.colorado.gov/cs/Satellite

Noddings, N. (1995). Teaching themes of care. *Phi Delta Kappan, 76,* 675–679.

Noguera, P. (2003). The trouble with black boys: The role and influence of environmental and cultural factors in the academic performance of African American males. *Urban Education, 38*(4), 431–459.

Noguera, P., & Yonemura, W. (Eds.). (2006). *Unfinished business: closing the racial achievement gap in our schools.* San Francisco: Jossey-Bass.

Olson, L. (2007). Gauging student learning: Quality counts. *Education Week, 26*(17), 42–44.

Orfield, G., & Yun, J. (1999). *Resegregation in American schools.* Cambridge, MA: Harvard University, Civil Rights Project.

Palmer, P. (1998). *The courage to teach: Exploring the inner landscape of a teacher's life.* San Francisco: Jossey-Bass.

Pewewardy, C. (1998). Fluff and feathers: Treatment of American Indians in literature and the classroom. *Equity & Excellence in Education, 31.* Retrieved from www.hanksville.org/storytellers/pewe/writing/Fluff.html—39k

Phillips, M., Crouse, J., & Ralph, J. (1998). Does the Black-White test score gap widen after children enter school? *American Educational Research Journal, 17,* 303–307.

Pollina, A. (1995). Gender balance: Lessons from girls in science and mathematics. *Educational Leadership, 53*(1), 30–33.

Ponterotto, J. G., Blanch, S., Greig, T., & Rivera, L. (1998). Development and initial score validations of the Teacher Multicultural Attitude Survey. *Educational and Psychological Measurement, 58,* 1002–1016.

Ponterotto, J. G., Mendelsohn, J., & Belizaire, L. (2003). Assessing teacher multicultural competence: Self report instruments, observer report evaluations, and a portfolio assessment. In D. B. Pope-Davis, H. Coleman, W. M. Liu, & R. L. Toporek (Eds.), *Handbook of multicultural competencies in counseling and psychology* (pp. 191–210). Thousand Oaks, CA: Sage.

Raphael, T. (1982). Question-answering strategies for children. *The Reading Teacher, 36*, 186–190.

Raphael, T. (1986). Teacher question-answer relationships, revised. *The Reading Teacher, 39*, 516–522.

Reigeluth, C. M. (1997). Educational standards: To standardize or to customize learning? *Phi Delta Kappan, 79*(3), 202. http://proquest.umi.com.ezproxy.library,wisc.edu/pqdweb?did=22080244&sid=1&Fmt=3&clientid=3751&RQT=309&VName=PQ

Rhode, D. L. (2006). *In pursuit of knowledge.* Stanford, CA: Stanford University Press.

Rocha, E., & Starkey, A. (2007). *Education: The state we're in.* Center for America Progress and Institute for America Future. Retrieved April 26, 2009, from http://www.america progress.org/site/pp.asp?c=biRJJ80VF&b=995593

Rose, L. C. (2002). NCLB: Failed schools—or failed law? No Child Left Behind: The mathematics of guaranteed failure. *Educational Horizon,* 121–130, November 20, 2008, Winter. Retrieved from http://www.pilambda.org/horizons/v82-2/Rose.pdf

Rothstein, R. (2004). *Class and school.* New York: Teacher College Press.

Schultz, B. (2008). *Spectacular things happen along the way: Lesson from an urban classroom.* New York: Teacher College Press.

Smith, N. J., Greenlaw, M. J., & Scott, C. J. (1987). Making the literate environment equitable. *Reading Teacher, 40,* 40–47.

Snyder, T., Tan, A. G., & Hoffman, C. M. (2004). *The digest of education statistics, 2003.* Washington, DC: U.S. Department of Education, National Center for Education Statistics.

Spencer, S. A., & Adams, J. D. (1990). *Life changes: Growing through personal transition.* San Luis Obispo, CA: Impact Publisher.

Strong, R., Silver, H. F., & Robinson, A. (1995). What do students want (and what really motivates them)? *Educational Leadership, 53*(1), 8–12.

Tatum, B. (1997). *Why are all the Black kids sitting together in the cafeteria? And other conversations about race.* New York: Basic Books.

Thompson, J. (1984). *Studies in theory of ideology.* Cambridge, UK: Polity Press.

Trow, W. C. (1960). Role functions of the teacher in the instructional group. In N. B. Henry (Ed.), *The dynamics of instructional groups* (pp. 61–78). Chicago: University of Chicago Press.

Wasserstein, P. (1995). What middle schoolers say about their schoolwork. *Educational Leadership, 53*(1), 41–43.

Watanabe, M., Nunes, N., Mebane, S., Scalise, K., & Claesgens, J. (2007). Chemistry for all, instead of chemistry just for the elite: Lessons learned from detracked chemistry classrooms. *Science Education, 91*(5), 683–709.

Weiner, L. (1993). *Preparing teachers for urban schools.* New York: Teachers College Press.

Weinstein, G., & Obear, K. (1992). Bias issues in the classroom: Encounters with the teaching self. In M. Adams (Ed.), *Promoting diversity in college classrooms: Innovative responses for the curriculum, faculty, and institutions* (pp. 39–50). San Francisco: Jossey-Bass.

Withhall, J. (1949/1960). Research tools: Observing and recording behavior. *Review of Educational Research, 30*(5), 496–512.

Wlodkowski, R. J., & Ginsberg, M. B. (1995). A framework for culturally responsive teaching. *Educational Leadership, 53*(1), 17.

Zeichner, K., & Liston, D. (1996). *Reflective teaching: An introduction.* Mahwah, NJ: Lawrence Erlbaum.

Zumwalt, K., & Craig, E. (2008). Who is teaching? Does it matter? In M. Cochran-Smith, S. Feiman-Nemser, D. J. McIntyre, & K. Demers (Eds.), *Handbook of research on teacher education: Enduring question in changing contexts* (3rd ed., pp. 404–423). New York: Routledge.

Index

CORWIN

A SAGE Company

The Corwin logo—a raven striding across an open book—represents the union of courage and learning. Corwin is committed to improving education for all learners by publishing books and other professional development resources for those serving the field of PreK–12 education. By providing practical, hands-on materials, Corwin continues to carry out the promise of its motto: **"Helping Educators Do Their Work Better."**